T0137499

SHATTERED NOT ABANDONED

Pastor Dr. Joan Rathe

WESTBOW
PRESS®
A DIVISION OF THOMAS NELSON
& ZONDERVAN

WestBow Press books may be ordered through booksellers or by contacting:

WestBow Press
A Division of Thomas Nelson & Zondervan
1663 Liberty Drive
Bloomington, IN 47403
www.westbowpress.com
1 (866) 928-1240

ISBN: 978-1-9736-7902-8 (sc)
ISBN: 978-1-9736-7904-2 (hc)
ISBN: 978-1-9736-7903-5 (e)

Library of Congress Control Number: 2019917826

Print information available on the last page.

WestBow Press rev. date: 11/20/2019

Contents

DEDICATION

This healing book is dedicated first and most importantly, to my Jesus, who watched, protected, and guided me through difficult challenges, trials, and circumstances. I'm so grateful for patient, merciful salvation, healing of my tortured body, and shredded soul.. I dream of your promises and am exhilarated in anticipation of becoming a part of your new world, where there will be no more tears shed, where I will be reunited with my loved ones,and dance on streets of gold eternally.

Lastly, I dedicate this book to my husband, Tom, who is my rock, soul-mate, and love of my life. Thank you for putting up with all the difficult and tragic times we experienced in our relationship and marriage. I know with certainty that this book will be life -changing for us, and I am so blessed and grateful to God that you and I will share these moments as we move forward to what God has ordained. I could have never completed what I have had it not been for your amazing faith in me and your unquenchable encouragement. You bring me love, hope, and joy for our brighter tomorrows serving Lord Jesus in unity.

ABOUT THE AUTHOR

Pastor Dr. Joan Rathe, recently becoming an ordained Pastor, is a Boston born strong native of Massachusetts presently residing in South Carolina with husband Thomas and Saint Bernard Puppy (Natalia Belle Joy AKA Tallie). Dr. Joan is credited as published Author of Sometimes it Rains Breaking Chains of Bondage - her Biography from victim to glory through faith in Jesus Christ. She is founder/CEO of a 501(c3) Charity breakingchainsfoundationandministry.org.The organization's mission focuses on reaching out to grieving families and victims caught up in chains of Grief and Loss, Addiction, Domestic Violence, Bullying, and all categories of Abuse. Dr. Joan received her Doctorate in Organizational Management and Leadership from University of Phoenix in 2009. She also holds one Master in Education and two other undergraduate degrees in fields of Music & Education. Dr. Joan is an accomplished singer/songwriter and her Album, "Beauty from Ashes" by GLORY can be purchased from I tunes, Amazon and additional sites internationally. Her new CD single *Shattered* written for her recent book (*Shatter Of Innocence*) won The Academia Music Award for best Christian Gospel in 2016. This CD or Book can be purchased through any of her sites. Dr.Joan works endlessly to promote stronger laws for victim*s rights in all states.

Prologue

If we are present on our planet long enough eventually, we will have an opportunity to grieve⁓ a lesson learned⁓ relative to trials based on tragic circumstances. Not one individual is likely to be excused from this common denominator as grief is woven like fine threads of silk into shades of life's purpose and tribulation. Grief⁓ without a doubt a strategic stronghold of a person's captivity according to depth, time-frame, and experience is planned ahead, and often without explanation. Rebellion, may br a primary mistake,which entails grief over unfortunate choices and walking away from Christ.

Christ uses grief for healing our broken and crushed spirit. No matter how we grieve, it is a natural emotion God brings to heal our broken souls. God is good and all He brings is good to encourage us who grieve for reasons beyond all our understanding. As we earn our lessons pressing into God, we recognize through him, we are healed of grief enabling positive outcome to emerge for benefit of Christ and ourselves. Simply stated, God loves us and uses our tragedy to strengthen us as prominent witnesses for His kingdom.

Words color our life and recommend various acceptance used in terms of grief, sharing, and healing. If you are a believer and a follower of Jesus, I pray today with all I have to give, that you uncover a presence of Christ you never realized existed. In addition, I pray that you will have abundant peace and exceeding joy as you develop an intimate and personal relationship with the Father, Son, and Holy Spirit. For the non-believer, my prayer is that you find God in the midst of this troubled world, embrace Him gladly, and follow His word in truth, dedication, and unconditional love.

My story has been told with to many tears and constant soaking prayer. My prayer for you is to open your doors of understanding, submit to God, and fully realize that each burden we carry encourages hope, deepens your faith in Christ, and insures your learned lesson in grief as God ordains. May God bless you and keep you, may His countenance shine on you and bring you peace beyond all understanding as you read these words God has placed on my grieving heart to share.

Part One : Fruits of the Spirit

Lessons Learned

Galatians 5:22 But The fruit of the spirit is love, joy, peace, forbearance, kindness, goodness, faithfulness, gentleness and self-control.

Galatians 5:23 Against such things there is no law.

There are of course those who may look at this scripture and want to debate these contents, but I was born with an extremely high inquiry of logic. which strongly governs my expectations of practicality and imagination. At the very least, these two often ignored attributes have become my control center for balance and growth throughout my lifetime objectives and achievements. Where unfilled? *Isaiah 32:17 the fruit of that righteousness will be peace; its effect will be quietness and confidence forever.*

Hmm- I wonder how this scripture adequately suits those who are mortally wounded from deep loss of a loved one and have no peace in their lives. Saying there is no peace unless you have faith with it may be a bit harsh. I have known many of strong faith fall on their face crying out to God in despair. One of the greatest hardships someone can experience in their lifetime is loss of a child. Not everyone with this dagger thrown in their heart walks away unscathed.

The trajectory of a beautiful life cut short with no explanation.

Where is the practical expectations of imagination we seek to baby step us through horrific nightmares? With each story I hear of a great loss draws my heart to the sufferer for I know only to well this familiar formula of combined emotions and guilt they are experiencing. Pain is unbearable and rationale is a mixture of denial and rage .Hope is only a word described in a dictionary and present is non-existent. Nothing remains but stinging guilt and failure.

In 2002 I lost my beautiful daughter Melanie Rachelle. We called her poopey for short- a name we affectionately gave her as a newborn. As she grew, her friends called her Mel but I called her Melanie- actually, Melanie Rachelle when she became a teenager. Melanie was extremely bright and challenging. Often, it became difficult to win an argument with her. Even teachers smiled when they spoke of how many times in class they felt that she was their teacher and they her students. With all her achievements, physical beauty, talent, and intelligence Melanie had a serious dark side. She was Bi-Polar and suffered from deep depression, bouts of Anorexia, Bulimia, and drugs, which ended her life to soon and turned me into an unimaginable zombie, who felt nothing but grief, guilt,and pain every day and night as I tried to live without her hugs, and walking beside me through life.

After Melanie"s burial, I left home in Salem, Mass for an extended trip through Canada hoping I might heal quicker if my mind was concentrating on beautiful Canada not sadness. Just like everything mesmerizing has to end, so did my escape from reality leaving me homeward bound locked in loneliness, sadness and a growing fear I would never recover. My sleeping habits became erratic. I either slept from morning to night or walked the floors all night long. Food was incidental to me.

I could have cared less about eating as I remembered my precious daughter fighting for control of her eating disorder and wishing there had been something more I could have done to help Melanie through her daily torment. Remembering her demons made me sick when I thought of food now an enemy to me. The most difficult thing I had to keep on hearing from friends, relatives, and people, who never knew her were comments like you need to give sadness some time, be patient with yourself. Can't tell you how many times I heard this told to me until I wanted to scream and punch walls.

Patience. What kind of patience was going to help me mend the hole in my heart for her? Patience was not going to give me Melanie back and peace is one of those emotional states that you will miss out on if you are not savvy about your directed course to embrace it. I had no clue how to capture this kind of peace. Where was this patience and peace I could not experience? Was I going to go through the rest of my life a basket case ending up in a mental institution completely shut up in an imaginative world where I could live my memories of Melanie? Was this what God had planned for me? Was this to be my epitaph?

When I started to think In terms of where could I go I was led to my computer. I heard a quiet voice inside directing me to a specific site. Although, I had no desire to use a computer at that moment something inside of me encouraged me to follow along. Soon I was looking at memorial sites sponsored by parents, who suffered great loss. Something inside me started to break. I found tears coming down my face faster than a rain forest shower. Falling to my knees I asked God to forgive me for blaming Him. At that moment,I knew I did not have to carry my cross of anger and guilt any longer. I had a purpose. I would build a memorial site and help others like Melanie and parents, who had suffered loss and remained stuck in their grief. That night Breaking Chains Foundation and Ministry was born and God gave me a peace I had never experienced before.

I had persecuted God, turned away from Him, and blamed Him for taking Melanie. I could not comprehend how much he loved me and accepted me unconditionally back in His arms until that moment I felt His grace touch me and received a peace beyond all understanding. Merciful God had in one moment in time reached down into the depths of my broken soul and quieted the raging storm within me. Tears poured down my face as this wayward daughter fell on her knees and prayed for the first time since Melanie had died. That night I slept for the first time and dreamed of angels standing by Melanie, who was laughing as she took a bite from her beloved apple. The Lord decides our lifespan. We need to guard our precious time here carefully as one that would watch over a sleeping infant. We need to gather every crumb of our life and be content with who we are and what we have. We may not always like a situation but remember,what God brings us to He will bring us through. His timing may be different from what we desire but he is faithful and will never leave us. Yesterday was gone and so was my precious daughter Melanie Rachelle, but I am grateful and blessed I had her in my lifetime. Today is the first day of my life and tomorrow may never come. I looked up, smiled and thought God has given me a great commission and now this would be my journey.

With a whirlwind of obligations, responsibilities, and deadlines to meet I dived face first into 2003 never stopping to look back determined and focused only on what I could achieve to minister to those who sought our ministry out. Breaking chains was now out there for the public to visit and I spent many days and nights answering distraught families and chained victims. Not long after I had gone public, messages from people began to pour in requesting my presence at a victims vigil, or speaking engagement in church, or another ministry project.

The greatest gift from God is His love and the greatest gift I could give Him was my faith in Him. I was now fully armored to begin my quest and put my faith to work through action. God is one force, who can obliterate mountains before us. Each one of us has experienced a mountain in their life preventing them from moving forward Their trials of fear, heartache, disease, disappointment, loneliness, homelessness, sorrow, and hurt have placed them in a cage bound by chains that prevent them from moving on. God's phone is never on a message unit, He is never on vacation and He is never late- in fact, He is always right on time. Our God is one contractor who can blow up all strongholds and clear our pathway forward. He is the one and only living God and we can reach Him anywhere 24/7. *Malachi 4:2 for you who revere my name, the sun of righteousness will rise with healing in its rays. And you will go out and frolic like well-fed calves.* Many instances we need to go strictly by faith alone and prayer tells us that through faith we will receive peace in our trampled lives. *2 Corinthians 5:7 "we live by faith not sight"*

We need to believe without question that we have the victory and stand firmly on that unfailing platform regardless of what we see, or hear. Stand still and wait on God to move. The reader must please understand here that our gracious God does not always answer us the way we would like Him to. Remember his will- not ours and although, we cannot understand why He does what He does- he is looking for the best path for his children no matter how difficult an answer may be. He has to live up to His character and truth is part of who He is. He does not change from past to present. " He is the same yesterday, today, and tomorrow." Yes, I had learned my lessons well.

Faith in God- our Alpha and Omega is certainly necessary for us to achieve patience in our lifetime circumstances. Developing patience of the Saints truly is a first step toward our attaining precious peace within our souls, a peace we seek, which poets write about, and dwells within the sleeping newborn. A peace that only God Almighty can give us. A peace beyond all understanding.

> *John 14:27 "Peace I leave with you; my peace I give you. I do not give to you as the world gives. Do not let your hearts be troubled and do not be afraid."*

Afraid- Was this what was chaining my body, mind, and spirit? Suddenly, emotions that had been tearing me apart for weeks began to make sense. More than anything, I realized when I sought out this bottomless pit I had fallen into that I was angry with Melanie for leaving me and I was being selfish wanting her back. Back to what? Most of her life was lived in terror and her body and mind were being destroyed by her dangerous lifestyle. I may not have understood why, but God in His infinite mercy had reached down and released her from bondage. He brought her home to \Him where she would finally be at peace and suffer no more.

In my confusion and loneliness I had turned my back on my faith.

I recognize now that I should have pressed closer to God for comfort and understanding. Jesus, my Savior never left me. He watched over me from a distance as I tried to find a rationale that suited my understanding and I completely missed the mark. His words ring clear in scripture.

> *Matthew 5:4 Blessed are those who mourn, for they will be comforted.*

> *Psalm 23:1 The Lord is my shepherd,I lack nothing*

I believe all these scriptures had a profound impact on my physical and mental welfare. God's compassion surrounded me. I no longer felt lost in space. My feet were solid on planet earth and my looking glass mirror was broken through as I stepped out from the maze and into light of His grace. There was hope and restoration and I knew in my heart God would be there walking beside me, guiding me on my path, and restoring my soul to life.

Months went by and although, there were deep bouts of depression, God was captain of my ship. I just sat back and let Him lead me through deep waters and unknown territory trusting Him with all my achievements, and disappointments. I was still in grieving stages, but I had placed my burden on God because I lost strength to carry this huge cross myself. I thought about how heavy His cross must have been as he dragged His tortured and broken body through the streets and then nailed to the cross He gave His life so we could be free~ Amazing Grace!!!!!. My tears clouded my eyes as I thought how He was carrying my cross because I could not. Once again, words called out to me from scriptures. *Psalm 55:22 Cast your cares on the Lord and he will sustain you;:he will never let the righteous be shaken.*

I knew my Father in Heaven was smiling down on me as He whispered "well done my good and faithful servant". "You have learned your lessons well". I believe I did. Patience and peace are linked together. There is no sign or separation of these two. In addition, they cannot be earned or bought. They are received only through faith. *Hebrews 11:1 Now faith is confidence in what we hope for and .assurance about what we do not see. We must believe by faith that God will reward those who earnestly seek him.* My heart was full. I looked forward to my next goal and stood still waiting patiently for God to show me my pathway.

"Peace is liberty in tranquility" –Cicero"

"Peace within makes beauty without"–George Herbert

Patience strengthens the spirit, sweetens the temper, subdues pride and bridles the tongue –George Math

Isaiah 26:3 you will keep in perfect peace those whose minds are steadfast, because they trusts in you.

Proverbs 14:30 A heart at peace gives life to the body, but envy rots the bones.

Romans 12:18 If it is possible, as far as it depends on you, live at peace with everyone.

If you go through each chapter of the Bible you will find many scriptures relative to peace. God's kingdom in Heaven is peace and His love never ends. Hallelujah!!!!!

"Where is Our Joy-Love"

I believe deep in my soul that Joy was the missing component for Melanie's happiness in life. So many times she would say in conversation. "What is wrong with me Mom" "am I broken" I would look at her in astonishment and say in a laughing manner. "Of course not Honey" "you are fine the way God meant you to be" Melanie would look at me with her beautiful Hazel eyes and ask -Then why can't I feel joy?" No matter what I do, I cannot find joy""I look for it all the time and can't feel it". Melanie and I had this conversation over and over, but she still could not experience joy talked about in sermon and I was unable to quiet her restless soul.. Joy is a form of happiness. The Bible tells us *Philippians 4:4 "Rejoice in the Lord always, I will say it again: Rejoice"*

In the words of Mathew W. Henry "Carnal joy puffs up the soul, but cannot fill it; therefore, in laughter the heart is sad."

True heavenly spiritual joy is filling to the soul; it has a satisfaction in it, answerable to the soul's vast and just desires. Thus does God satiate and replenish the weary soul. Nothing more than the desire of this joy is desire of the soul. I truly believe Melanie never experienced this form of amazing joy".

Walking away from the Lord certainly held no joy for me. I was moody, argumentative, depressed and very jealous of any family that came into my frame of view where there was a little girl who reminded me of my daughter. Between my crying jags and depression I had become hopeless filled to the brim with pain and condemnation. Merciful God met me where I was at- lifted me from murky waters and gave me a purpose. How great is our God!

> *Psalm 16:11 You make known to me the path of life; you will fill me with joy in your presence, with eternal pleasures at your right hand. "Lead us O God; from the lovely things of the world to the thought of you the creator; and grant that while we delight in the beautiful things of your creation we may delight in you. The first author of beauty and the Sovereign Lord of all your works, blessed forever more"* (George Appleton)

> *1 Peter 1:8 Though you have not seen him, you love him; and even though you do not see him now, you believe in him and are filled with an inexpressible and glorious joy*

> *Psalm 28:7 The Lord is my strength and my shield ; my heart trusts in him, and helps me. My heart t leaps for joy, and with my song I praise him.*

When we compare Joy vs Happiness. Joy and happiness are both wonderful feelings to experience; but are very different in emotional impact. Joy arrives when you find inner peace within yourself and recognize who,what, and why you are,whereas happiness tends to be externally triggered and is based on other places, people, thoughts and events . It becomes challenging for all of us facing grief to completely change our mindset from negative influences to that of Joy. There are three specific methods to incorporate in your daily schedule to increase your territory in the amount of Joy you bring into your life First and most importantly be there and do not seek out ways to avoid being there working on your grief. Meditation first thing in the morning is an excellent choice to begin your day schedule. Prayer and simple stretching body movements pulls your whole self into a peaceful and relaxed state and God will walk along with you through the maze.

Secondly. Forget the media. There is no joy listening to who murdered who that morning. Your mind is already in a state of peril why place a further drama on yourself? Instead, have breakfast outside if weather is good, listen to music that is calming to your soul, take a brief walk, run. or a short bike ride.

Finally- shower, dress, list your priorities and errands, and go forth my friend in joy and harmony. Time and people are precious gifts from God. Enjoy them and be proud of who you are. Refuse to accept negativity, wishing, or worrying. Be that special person- not someone who brings everyone down by their discontented soul. When you don't know what to say-say nothing. Just let your quiet presence be a powerful witness to your love. Your presence is worth much more than words.

Your presence communicates to the other that he or she is valued, precious, beloved. Your presence brings not only the gift of yourself into the relationship but also, in and through you, the gift of God. How many times I cried out to God asking the same question. Why? I am quite sure God was as tired of hearing me ask him the same old question daily as I was hearing people tell me be patient. When Melanie left this world it was Easter morning. I was sure that when

I stopped life support God would save her as he did for Lazarus in the Bible. When this did not happen and her heart stopped beating I was frozen in time.

Why did he not save Melanie? It was Easter. God saved Lazarus. God did answer me that day. Melanie was not Lazarus. Shock to reality. That was why. Melanie was not Lazarus therefore, no miracle would take place. Wow! That was a wake-up call for me. After that, when people would ask me why don't I have the courage. faith, endurance, and patience of Job? I looked back at them, smiled, and answered – "I am sorry but I am not Job" Joy in life really is a choice. "Don't squander one bit of this marvelous life God has given us".

Joyful, joyful, we adore thee

God of glory, God of love;
Hearts unfold like flowers before thee,
Opening to the sun above.

(Henry Van Dyke) (1852)

How beautiful is this first stanza of his lovely work. You read those captivating words and one cannot help but feel exceeding joy in praising our creator. A joy that pales in comparison to just a fleeting moment of happiness. Joy in abundance- everlasting, irreplaceable, and at times incomprehensible joy.We truly miss the greatness of joy when we seek to settle for those fleeing seconds of happiness. The New International edition of the Holy Bible shows the word Joy 155 times in the New Testament and 63 times in the Old Testament. Caught up in our drama we tend to allow ourselves second hand happiness.

Joy is to profound to ever be confused with superficial happiness. You don't have to wait for a crisis to occur in your life for you to experience the joy that a single prayer offers. Even the smallest detail is of importance to God. There is a welcome joy one experiences in prayer. Prayer is the gentle cover of our book of life. If it becomes dusty from lack of usage then we have no-one to blame but ourselves. A difficult lesson to learn but sometimes facing truth is always the most critical reality a person faces.

There was not a drop of emotional joy within me after I lost Melanie and there was certainly no prayer. Thinking back if I had learned; no- if I had known true joy I would have been on my face praying to God, instead of using my anger lashing out at Him for her death. I would have understood that Melanie made these choices and that He was merciful bringing her home.

God protected her from her own demons and released her soul to rest. As her mom, I was deeply wounded, but because I had walked away from God I could not grasp the reality of the circumstances.

There was only one thing that kept me from joy and that was denial. I was stuck in denial in every aspect of my life as to the reasons behind her death. I lived in a kind of looking glass existence for years believing my explanation and creating a rationale for it all. There was no joy in understanding the truth. I simply lost my way and an opportunity to move forward in my own area. All I had known as truth was not and all that I had believed not was true. The answer was harsh when it hit home. Melanie had made her choice to die and she alone went down that never returning path.

The source of joy is illustrated when Jesus says, "*These things have I spoken unto you that my joy might remain in you and that your joy might be full.*" The joy of a Christian is the joy of Jesus.

Voltaire never believed in God and said before he died, "I wish I had never been born". Joy of Jesus is constant. It does not flit from person to person as the Bumble Bee does from flower to flower. Joy of Jesus is drawn into the heart and remains within you.

We all have trials and crosses to carry. God gives us the oil of joy for mourning. At the very hour of mourning Jesus pours in the oil of His joy. Jesus plants his garden and we are the vines. As vines grow, a Gardner will need to insure that there are no twisted vines or branches that could break off and never bear fruit. The fruit is very vital to the Gardner being able to fulfill his planting. The fruit of the vine he cultivates in turn and we receive a continual joy from Jesus and without joy of Jesus, our sufficiency of joy will never be filled.

Amazing Grace- He is certainly all of that.1 John, 4:16 And so we know and rely on the love God has for us. God is love. Whoever lives in love, lives in God,, and God in them. Our joy in the Lord is Amazing Grace. It stretches like a rubber band around our lives and reaches deeper than the ocean and wider than space in time. An anchor springing up from a foundation of circumstances through our God, our one constant in our struggles.

> *Jude 1:24 To him who is who is able to keep you from stumbling and to present you before his glorious prescence without fault and with great joy-*

I should have been better informed about joy when Melanie posed her question to me. I was disappointed I had failed Melanie with a brief explanation and laughing to quiet her soul when I should have taken pains to minister to my anxiety ridden daughter. I believe I would have smiled and replied " Melanie, joy is in the Lord- The more we press into him the more joy we receive." Joy can only be multiplied when it is divided." I most likely would have then recited the second verse from

> *Henry Van Dyke's song of joy.*
> *Melt clouds of sin and sadness; drive the dark of doubt away;*
> *Giver of immortal gladness; Fill us with the light of day*
> *I should have told her as she walked out that fated day*

Thessalonians 5:16 Be joyful always. I know with certainty Melanie would have kissed my cheek and whispered, "thanks Mom"

What does love look like? I believe that is a question of the ages. If you take the perspective of Christian and look at the word love there are multi usages of that emotion. First, we should establish that love is an emotion and not just a condition as I love pizza, I love the beach, I love music. All these are tailored to the condition of a feeling or an attraction. It does not have hands to help others, nor does not have feet to hasten to the poor and needy .This does not have eyes to see misery and want, nor does it ever hear the sighs and sorrows of men. All this is needed to establish a special and specific emotion of love,because all this is the very essence of what love truly means.

Love has been said to be capable of unification of people. This form of love would completely fulfill their every need. Love joins connecting people by whatever is deepest in their soul and combines their emotions as one .Love is lifted up in many religious events by *1 Corinthians 13:4-5 Love is patient, Love is kind, it does not envy, it does not boast, it is not proud, it is not rude, it does not dishonor others it is not self-serving, it is not easily angered, it keeps no wrongs or rights.*

> *1 Corinthians 13:1 If I speak in the tongues of men or of angels, but do not have love, I am only a resounding gong or a clanging cymbal. If I have the gift of prophecy and can fathom all mysteries and all knowledge, and if I have a faith that can move mountains, but do not have love, I am nothing. If I give all I possess to the poor and give over my body to the hardship that I may boast, but do not have love, I gain nothing.*

> *1 Corinthians 13:13 And now these three remain: faith, hope and love. But the greatest of these is love.*

Being there showing the other person you are engaging in something they are interested in is good way to express admiration. Being involved and doing the right thing correctly is more than admiration, It represents what real love and commitment are .

Love was the only thing I could offer Melanie. I could not take away her horrific pain of depression and was clueless on how to mentor her when she would experience one of these attacks. Most of the time, when she had an episode, she was nowhere to be found- so even if I had wanted to help her- I could not. I realized to late that love when it was just used as a word could do nothing. There had to be outstretched hands cradling this labor of love and embraced by the other person as well for healing power of love to withstand these trials of life. Love is God's essence, power His attribute; therefore, is His love greater than His power?

This question seems to capture God's great ability by illustrating how powerful His love is for us. His very essence is love, therefore, we can receive this grace from God by pressing in to Him every opportunity. We have that incredible offer available to us any time we require loving arms . The Lord clearly states this in scripture.

John 3:16 God so loved the world that he gave his one and only son,that whoever believes in him shall not perish, but have eternal life. Our heavenly Father loves us, for he allows us to be called his children, and we really are! There is no one like him. You can search this world through and through but you will never find anyone who loves you like he does. Unconditional love that knows no boundaries or end. We know how much God loves us, and we have put our trust in him.

> *1 John 4:16 And so we know and rely on the love God has for us. God is love. Whoever lives in love lives in God. I in them.*

> *Lord, I thank you for your love. Grant that I will love others as you do. Freely, completely, selflessly,*

> *and in loving others, may I spread your praise from shore to shore! Amazing Grace how sweet the sound, that saved a wretch like me, I once was lost, but now I'm found, I was blind but now I see.*

Those were the very first words I ever heard which lead me to God. I was in my car driving and I heard the most incredible music I had ever heard . It was as if I was surrounded by a choir of angels.

The music seemed distant and so I reached out to adjust my car radio but the volume was still very low. I thought it might be the station and tried to change it, but every one I tried had that same music playing. I am not one to jump to conclusions, but I clearly had no say in changing my listening options. Then I realized the music was not coming out of my radio speakers. This incredible sound was in my ears and head. I had never had that experience before and so I was shocked Hitting my head with my hands trying to block my ears had no effect. The music played on and on. I thought I was losing my mind. As the music grew louder a voice sounded in the middle calling me by my name saying that God was with me and this would be our symbol of communication when He required my attention..

I would know with certainty He was with me and directing my path. I don't know if I was happy or frozen with fear when I heard his voice but I was not going to refuse my assignment in anyway shape of form.. When he called I had better be ready for the call. After that experience, the first call came at 2:00 am in the morning where I was given names to pray for for one hour. I did not know any of these people, but I prayed my heart off. This intercession continued night after night. I was surprised I was not more tired than I was. I seemed to have more energy than before when I was sleeping through the night .I found that as a servant of God, you develop major endurance and energy.

After my prayers He began to dictate words to me. I would write as fast as I could so as not to miss one thing. Sometimes, I would be sleeping and God would wake me and send me to my keyboard to play music. Once again, I would obey and soon I was writing the first song I had ever written. It was called The Greatest Gift is Love" and became the title of my first album. I felt blessed. At this time I was attending a small church and one morning I heard Amazing Grace. God told me to start singing it and walk toward the Worship team.. Although, I did not want to stand out, I obeyed and began to move forward singing.

The worship team asked me to come up and stand with them and sing . I graciously accepted their offer. Within two days, I was asked to join their team permanently, which I faithfully served on for three years. During that time I lost Melanie. There was not a dry eye in my church at her funeral. The team honored Melanie with all her favorite Christian songs and people of the church brought in so much food the selection was endless. I was grateful for the compassion and grace extended to me and my family. I will always remember that night with God's arms holding and rocking me as I went through a service I never ever expected- death of my daughter.

Denial almost destroyed me and. had it nor been for my precious Lord I would still be in a dead stop as one stops on a Ferris wheel to let passengers off. There was no stop for me. I was in limbo stuck between reality and make believe. There was no turning back and I could not move forward. My life seemed hopeless and stripped of value .Our precious Savior was always there close to me watching and protecting me. Because I had listened to his voice and had become an obedient child he reached down and lifted me up from my pit of darkness and set me high on dry land filling my mind with visions of things to come.

> *Luke 11:28 He replied " Blessed rather are those who hear the word of God and obey it."*

Lord, hear my" prayer. Lord please teach me to recognize your voice. Times I am weary and my ears hear nothing. Please help me to focus on just you. I too like men and women of the Bible desire to hear your voice- so please speak. I will train my ears to listen for you and become accustomed to the sound of your call. Amen.You are holy, Lord, the only God. And your deeds are wonderful. You are great, you are the most high. You are Almighty. You, holy Father, are King of heaven and earth.

You are three and one, Lord God, all good. You are good,all good, supreme good. Lord God, living and true. You are love, You are wisdom, You are endurance, You are rest. You are peace, you are joy and gladness, You are all our riches, and you suffer for us. You are beauty, You are gentleness, You are our protector,You are our guardian and defender. You are courage, You are our heaven and our hope You are our Lord, our great consolation, You are our eternal life, great and wonderful Lord, God Almighty, merciful Savior. (Saint Francis of Assisi.)

Dear God, Speak to my children in their hearts. Imprint your voice on their memories that they may learn to discern your voice from the voice of others. Amen. 2003 sped by quickly and I spent time writing,teaching,speaking, and building a firm foundation for Breaking Chains Memorial. My focus was now on my other two daughters Lauren and Riva. Somehow I thought with Melanie gone things would move on finally and all of us could find peace at last as we fought to establish a new foundation in our shattered lives.

> *Nahum 1-9 Whatever they plot against the Lord he will bring to an end; trouble will not come a second time.*

As incredibly busy as I was with ministry,I remained true to my field of education teaching children and young adults. 2004 arrival was on the way- fast and furious. I remember the snow and the ice came early that year. I had recently signed a contract as Music Supervisor for an elementary school not far from my home. I was excited about the position and looked forward to bringing my expertise to a very old fashioned music program.. The other teaching staff were stellar and everyone pitched in to aide me with all the new children to help make everybody feel comfortable and transition well.

My husband and I spent a quiet thanksgiving that year as we remembered Melanie. Absent from our table were both of my parents who had passed away two years before Melanie did. The bird was cooked the sweet aroma of thanksgiving was all around us but there was no spirit of love and excitement as in the past. Our loss was immeasurable. We never forgot at that meal to praise and thank God for our good fortune with my new teaching position. We thanked \ Him for our health and our foo before us. There was an additional reward that holiday. I had four paid days off plus the weekend and Tom did as well. God's love blessed two of \His lost children struggling for peace and joy.

I returned to my teaching duties and for the most part began planning a Christmas Concert for the school. The children were all excited about their solos and group performances. They were thrilled to come to Music class. There was more interest than misbehaving and I for one, was happy that my job had become easier, and filled with excitement and fun for myself. Each classroom was busy making costume and scenery to compliment the concert. Excitement was in the air as teachers, parents, and myself helped in creating an amazing Christmas performance.

The date of the concert was two days before winter vacation began, which afforded me enough time for all my errands outside of school. This concert for our last day of school was followed by refreshments, class parties, and exchanging gifts. Children and parents were so excited over our successful concert - a never before production- parents, teachers, along with my supervisors congratulated my outstanding school concert efforts. I smiled as I humbly accepted beautiful Roses and thundering applause. Each class showered me with beautiful gifts and I felt blessed that everyone liked me and our first production. My mind flitted as I thought another two weeks paid vacation. I looked up and thanked God. for all blessings. I wish my parents and Melanie could have been there, but you are and you dear God are all I need. Amen!

Christmas was coming and I was on vacation. Most of my Christmas shopping was finished including wrapping gifts, which is one job I prefer not to, but a necessary chore for anyone shopping-I I was prepared at last for my Christmas season.. Sometimes, I was fortunate to find a store that wrapped for free, but more stores began to charge for the privilege of wrapping and I had to suck it up- as we all do- and do my own.

I spent my free time between church and family sharing quality time with my oldest daughter, Lauren. We shopped, laughed about silly things, cooked, and ate our meals together. Lauren mourned hard when she lost Melanie. They were best friends from the time they were young, and Lauren, typical big sister when Melanie was born, always played that role, even as they grew to young adults. Protective and loving Lauren watched out for Melanie, even when she put her own life in danger. There was nothing she would not do for her little sister and Melanie adored her. Lauren had always been my right hand for whatever I needed,, whether it was putting a shelf together, or shopping with me for the right color contacts.. she excelled in all she tried and her school grades were excellent. I felt blessed and proud of her.

Against all odds, she received not one, but three degrees. Her first achievement was in Juvenile Justice, second was Political Science, and her third degree was Acting. I would joke about her complex schooling and answer people by saying " Lauren is a professional student". I never dreamed she would set her course to return for a strong nursing program, but she did- and four years later she graduated as an RN. from Salem State College School of Nursing. At the time of her graduation, she was Mom of two young boys and in process of a messy divorce.

Lauren worked difficult assignments. One of her shifts, working with incarcerated addicts serving their needs. Lauren began using drugs plus prescribed medication for depression and pain.. Not long after my special Christmas week with Lauren, I was hit from behind- as a truck you never see coming. Satan sliced into my life once again, and on 12/17/04 Lauren was found in her apartment dressed in her scrubs keeled over. She had been dead for four days and to this day we do not understand any of the mysterious circumstances of her strange and untimely death..

Our teaching staff planned to get together at a local restaurant that night for a staff celebration. No-one was prepared for my telephone call that evening to apologize for not being able to make their gathering because my Daughter, Lauren had been found dead in her apartment. I remember barely going through motions or moving as I called teachers and explained my daughter had died. Everyone was dumbfounded. They knew I had lost Melanie, but now another Daughter. They were unable to comprehend my horrific loss.

I then got into my car completely oblivious to any other car on the road and drove to my friend's home and collapsed in her arms. My short drive seemed endless and I knew God was the only one,who safely saw me there, ministered to me, and stayed till I fell asleep. Next morning was like a bad dream. I could not function, I thought it was a nightmare, but when reality set in when I stopped screaming- I was numb, void of any and all emotion. I just sat and stared into space wanting to die. My friend tried to get some food into me, but I was nauseated and could not eat.

How could this be happening again. My second daughter was another victim for death. What happened here ? Trouble had once more arrived and my beautiful Lauren was gone forever I cannot describe my anguish at that moment. There must be a mistake . They had the wrong person, after all, the body had decayed . Maybe another woman-maybe a friend was staying there with her. I must of thought of at least twelve variables for error but in the end – there it was. All my denial in this world would not alter truth and that was Lauren was gone. My mind began to race in multi directions, yet, I remained motionless on my friend's sofa. Who would tell Riva her only sibling left had died? I thought of my youngest daughter and I knew, without a doubt, I could not shoulder that heart wrenching responsibility. .

I had to make arrangements for Lauren, and who would tell Lauren's ex husband? He would have to break the news to their two young sons. My mind wondered and reflected back to my teaching position I had just started. Everybody will be so upset. I pondered through the many questions concerning my new contract.. Would I be let go after all, I was still new on their staff. Music was important for their curriculum. Until I arrived, there was no music hour in place, which made it impossible for teachers to execute planning and break time. .what would everyone now do??? So much to do and I did not know where to begin. Tears streaming down so fast I could not see. I felt a strong arm around me but there was no one there. I knew it was God and He was taking my burden, which had become to heavy now for me to lift.

I wanted to ask him why- why Jesus my daughter? I stopped that question before I asked knowing that after Melanie why was not important. What was important and my one save is the love of God filling me with peace and love beyond all measure. All my many concerns were soon answered. Tom had gone to tell Riva and called those who needed to know at that moment. Lauren's ex husband was devastated and began his difficult task telling their young sons, who loved their Mom and found it hard to understand why they would not see her in their life any more. Saying goodbye to one daughter had been devastating for me,but how does one say goodbye to a second child ?

The week was long and I walked into so many walls of protocol. First, I could not have Lauren. She was still married and her husband had all decisions to make, not our family. Then, I had to look for him because Lauren and he were no longer together at the time she died. That was additional stress I certainly did not need. I had difficulty financially as members of my family helped me secure a proper burial for Lauren. Getting everything in place was an additional period of endless waiting and depression. With all the twists and turns her funeral was as perfect as I could arrange,and Lauren was at last at rest with her sister Melanie.

We held a small gathering after the funeral and people, friends, and neighbors began stopping by . I tried to hold up through the many hugs of sympathy but could not and several instances I lost my strength and broke down crying. Several teachers came to pay their respects and even my principal was there at the funeral. I was a little surprised but felt blessed when one of the teachers told me that the principle wanted to assure me my position with them would be there when I returned. I was also told to return when I was ready and I would be paid in full while I remained absent.

Thank you God for the wonderful family of teachers I had at that time. Thank you for all the compassion and helping hands they lent to me when I returned five weeks later. Had I not been in such an amazing school position- I don't believe I would have bounced back as quickly as I did. Thank you Jesus for all you gave me at that horrific time in my life. You brought me to it and you brought me through it. Your love is what kept me sane and you are my all in all. Amen.

1John 4:18 there is no fear in love. But perfect love drives out fear, because fear has to do with punishment . The one who fears is not made perfect in love

He is truly Amazing Grace. To have faith in God will lead you to recognize faith in yourself. Faith will build a trust in God and when trials appear in your doorway you will rest and be confident that God will bring you through your storm. I began building my foundation in faith and trust in God when Melanie died. I believe my growth those past two years enabled me to meet my second great loss. Although broken, confused and heartsick over Lauren, I was able to push on quicker because I was a strong believer, and had a ministry to tend to.

Not everyone recovers at the same rate or under the same circumstances. Each story of loss and grief is unique because the loss belongs to them. Everyone will face a loss during their life span— some greater than others, but there is one constant through this maze, which is the love of God for his children. Even if your faith is small as a mustard seed God will reach out and assist you with your Christian growth. Faith is within our belief system. As Christians we fully understand

> *Proverbs 3:5-6 trust in the Lord, with all my heart, and lean not on my own understanding.; In all your ways submit to him, and he will make your paths straight.*

Believe me when I tell you I have ed over and over my way and fallen flat on my face. I learned my lesson well concerning faith in God Remember the tiny mustard seed I referred to . I f you can muster up that wee amount of faith in God you will move mountains and strongholds in your life right out of your path.

> *Hebrews 11:1 now faith is confidence in what we hope for and assurance about what we do not see.*

Has the Lord brought you to a small territory in life? If He has you must be grateful and blessed. You must care for it because that small gift is yours from God but always remember the real landlord to your plot in life belongs to God. Has the Lord brought you to a large territory? This too must be watched over with great care for this also belongs to God.

You soon learn that God increases our territory when he sees how faithful we remain to our gift large or small. We must accept, be content, and do good with what is given to us because everything given is his- not ours True faith has no doubt. There is absolutely no possibility of having doubt in your heart if you are a believer and trust God in every circumstance.

When we lift our hands in prayer and then walk away thinking I hope God hears me, I hope God does not leave me, I hope I don't lose my home. These statements all reflect doubt in what you just prayed. God cannot move with doubt because that is not a characteristic of his character. God is truth, faithful, and loving. To allow doubt after he receives prayer forces him to hold back his blessing.

You cannot step up to the plate and refuse to play in the game. *James:1-6, but when you ask, you must believe and not doubt, because the one who doubts is like a wave of the sea, blown and tossed by the wind.*

I love that God is so receptive to our needs when we are faithful to his. There is nothing we cannot ask if it is in His will, then we will receive our blessing. do with Almighty God by our side. There is nothing he cannot handle- all we have to do is bring our prayers to Him and then sit back and watch God move. Remember that when we are faithful in little things God will bless us with more. Our God is an awesome God.

Lord, thank you for being so faithful. We never have to ask twice. You are always preparing things before we ask. Your measure of grace is extraordinary none can duplicate. You are truly our God,who loves us wherever and whatever are our circumstances. We are a chosen generation and you are our supreme Father of all. Amen. Looking back in retrospect, I clearly visualize many lessons that we face in a lifetime.. Each time, we succeed in understanding rationale behind our actions,we begin to see the forest for the trees. Time becomes an endless " continuum of pathways, some narrow and unlit as we blindly stumble through our maze. Yet, do not lose faith for the scriptures assure us that every step will be guided by Almighty God.

James 1:17 Every good and perfect gift is from above, coming down from the Father of the heavenly lights, who does not change like shifting shadows.

Thank you Lord, for your light of truth and compassion, which makes our way safe and sweet. With the light of your presence, you warm my mind. With the light of your word you illuminate my path to go forward.

Psalm 19: 105 Your word is a lamp for my feet, a light on my path.

Psalm 40:5 Many, O Lord my God. Are the wonders you have done. The things you planned for us. none can compare with you. Were I to speak and tell of your deeds, they would be to many to declare.

When I think of my past mistakes and realize that I never could have become victorious in my trials had God himself not touched me with his hand of mercy and lifted me to safe ground. You God are the one I trust and know you are watching me always.

God's love is immeasurable, inexhaustible, inescapable, irrepressible, insatiable, irrational. O Lord, my deepest desire is to know more of you and recognize your love through personal experience, and in my limited capacity to be filled from your unlimited resources. Amen!

Psalm 103-8:11 The Lord is compassionate and gracious, slow to anger, abounding in love. He will not always accuse, nor will He harbor His anger forever. He does not treat us as our sins deserve, or repay us for our iniquities. For as high as the heavens are above the earth, so great is His love for those who fear Him.

I firmly believe God's love sustained me through those endless years following Melanie and Lauren's death. Love mixed with joy replaced mourning for Lauren to gladness and dance we did as Tom and I renewed our marriage vows in a lovely ceremony in Calvary Church Lynn-field, Massachusetts before close friends and family.

I returned to my teaching position with Winthrop Schools, Massachusetts. Maybe it was the explosion of love from my small students, which showered over me incentive to create and seek higher knowledge. I enrolled at University of Phoenix Doctoral Program in one of their most difficult high paced on-line Courses. There were speaking engagement schedules I had never encountered before. Between personal, professional,and educational responsibilities I had little time to fully concentrate on my loss. Oh, and did I mention, I had 13 active Saint Bernard puppies to take care of, who had just lost their Mother, Mischa.

Tom and I took turns at night watching over our little ones and during the day when we both worked we had a wonderful Nanny. Although, we were active in our church and busy all the time, we could not shake off sadness and memories of Melanie and Lauren surrounding us everywhere we went. With time passing quickly, it wasn't long before puppies were growing like weeds and a crowd favorite attraction to busy passers by. Our Salem, Massachusetts home was a corner lot directly across from Forrest River Park and beach. Every day, thousands of people passed our home on the way to the park or beach for a family outing or a sports event especially, Salem State college students, whose dormitories locale was in our area.

Our beautiful dogs, who I individually named soon attracted authorities. There was a regulation of no more than three dogs and we had 13. We decided to relocate and Tom and I moved South never knowing what would prove multiple significant loss to bear. We had made several attempts to relocate to Myrtle beach, South Carolina to be near friends. Nothing panned out and we decided to wait on another opportunity knowing we were short on time, because we had been given a deadline to move the dogs, sell them, or lose them. We found a builder on-line as well as a Realtor and after several visits to Carolina we gave a deposit of 10,000 to have the builder construct our home.

We were turned around to South Carolina country, instead of Myrtle Beach, but no matter- we were going to be able to keep our dogs and build our dream home at the same time.

We sought God as to what we should do and as doors were being opened for us we knew we were going forward. Five months after our telephone calls back and forth with the builder we had a beautiful home and area to bring our Saints. Knowing we were moving, made our situation bearable however, I did not want to wait and devised ed a plan to ship all our dogs to South Carolina to wait for us. I only wish I had seen what would be the result of my decision as I would have never let them go without us. We found a small farm in the area, where we could board our dogs and after medical clearance, birth information and any special notes all but one Saint headed South with a young man, who was employed by our vet and knew our puppies well..

We turned our focus to packing belongings we would be bringing ourselves, hired movers, gave our resignations to employers, placed our home on sale, and went to do a walk through our new home. When we arrived, the home was not anything like we had planned, but we were stuck in a hard place with no other options. The contract had been signed and a date to complete our sale was right in our face. We had to sell our Salem residence to pay for our new home and the clock was winding down to zero hour. In addition to all this drama returning home, we found that our dogs in South Carolina were being neglected. We enlisted the aide of an organization to get the dogs away from there at once. The director was a strict woman and refused to return our dogs. After pleading with her, she agreed to give us back two of our Saints. We chose the father and the twin of my female Saint.

We had a buyer and were thrilled to be finally leaving all painful memories behind us. We sold our home in 15 days in the dead of Winter right before Christmas holiday but our South Carolina builder sold our home from under us, because he was not assured we would be able to sell our home and refused to honor the 24 hour extension we had placed on the contract. He also refused to return our 10,000 deposit explaining there was nothing in the contract that indicated a return if he sold it within that 24 hour period and we failed to meet that obligation. We had sold the house- we had a deposit, but the builder would not accept payment.

Our new owners of our Salem house pushed us out and would not extend our time to find another\home. We flew to Carolina and with the help of an area Realtor bought the first home, which proved to need updating. We headed South with three of our Saints in one of the most blinding snow storms that hit that night and lasted two days as we moved on toward a new beginning.

KINDNESS: PEACE: ANOTHER QUESTION?

Kindness. according to the concordance means brotherly. The greatest thing a person can do for his heavenly Father is to be kind to some of his other children. Two of the greatest commandments are first- to love thy God with all thy heart, soul,mind,and strength and second greatest commandment is to love thy neighbor as you love thyself. To many times, the second commandment is ignored or interpreted as wished. This clearly shows that people don't understand or care enough about themselves to be able to return kindness and love to others. .Kindness cannot be measured in dollars and cents, nor can it be found in selfishness. To be sure, kindness to others will reap benefit,s but not in pay- for kindness pays most when you do not earn any pay for it. How simple and profound that is when you repeat it aloud and how beautiful in meaning.

> *Kindness is loving people more than they deserve. (Joseph Joubert)*

I'm quite sure that during the course of our lifetime we meet one person,who fits this description, but because we obey and honor God's wishes we acknowledge this unpleasant person with kindness.

Well, I believe in the old adage do unto others as you would have them do unto you. When I lost my daughters, I was full of bitterness and enough heat to cook a lean cuisine. There was not one single person, place,or thing that filled my desire to care enough. The simple truth was I could not even stand being with myself.

I was riddled and tormented with guilt and anger, and try as I would- nothing made sense in this world. I did not care who was right, or who was wrong. .Everyone was giving opinions,which I did not ask for. Their kindness was interpreted by me as meddling and I did not appreciate, or want their comments during my mourning period. I stayed alone many times and thought about the good years .I finally realized that I had much to be grateful for and I had been truly blessed to have shared so many years as their Mom.

I recognized that true worth is in being and not just seeming to accomplish things as days fly by. I learned some little good is not in just well wishing, or dreams of accomplishments in days ahead. .I saw whatever men hold close as kindness in-spite of desires of youth-there is nothing as royal as kindness, and nothing more precious than truth..Compassion will most certainly be the antidote in curing more sins than condemnation. *Romans 8:1 Therefore, there is no condemnation in Christ Jesus.*

The world of kindness does not stand alone by any means. Kindness requires the ultimate touch of gentleness. Our world can never go amiss in bestowing gentleness to all people. There is no day when it is untimely, and,no place where it will not find grace. Gentleness will never do harm, but every gentle act may save a life from hopelessness. Dear God, today I pray that my heart be gentle and reach and minister to all afflicted with loss. Thank you for granting me my deep desire for restoration of lost souls. Amen!

When we enter God's kingdom in prayer and approach his throne room you become aware of his power, grace, kindness, gentleness, and introduced to three principles of gentleness which surround our God'. First, and most importantly, there is nothing stronger than his gentleness, secondly, we learn from experience that power melded with gentleness will accomplish more than intimidation and violence, and lastly,you are kind to yourself when you show God's gentleness with others. These are definitely three rules to consider as you trudge down rough roads of life.. Our God is faithful and will never leave us. What my amazing revelation was during those difficult circumstances,\encountered through trials was man will always disappoint you, but amazing God never will. He is always there at just the right time with the right solution to your need.

Sometimes, we do not agree with God's decision, but there is always a well thought out rationale regarding his choices for our life. After all, he is the only one, who knows the big picture of our existence, but he bestows on us ability to chose freely. No matter what path we decide, God protects you by closing doors to warn you when you need to rethink your decision, and opening doors and windows to let you know your on the right track full steam ahead. If you follow his blueprint you are going to have victory. Without it, you will be in places that will ultimately bring you destruction, and failure.

As we approach Him daily, willing to be molded, reshaped, and directed, His word brings us guideposts of clear direction. Almost everything we read, see, and experience reveals to us in some way that, although, we do not visibly see God, He is always watching over us, In our quiet times, God will reach out to us and open doors to our heart releasing our creativity and filling us with His glory. That is how God approached me. All my written books and music came to me inspired by Almighty God. Through my prayer and sweet dreams from cover to finish His glory is acknowledged and I am only His faithful sheep,who brought my Great Shepherd the recognition He deserved.

Dreams are the ultimate connection God uses to message us. Sometimes, we choose to ignore our dreams if they were powerful and frightening, but do not be afraid. Every dream we have in some way holds a message from All Mighty God for us. At times, the meaning may appear muddled or tragic, but if you remember in the Bible not everyone, who had a dream or vision received good news but always informative,

Genesis 28:12 (Jacob) had a dream in which he saw a staircase resting on the earth with its top reaching to heaven, and the angels of God were ascending and descending on it.

Genesis 37:5 Joseph had a dream, and when he told it to his brothers,they hated him all the more. Some of our dreams prove to be disappointing, but these are "wishful thinking " dreams, things we come up with our own minds, circumstances, or situations we wish would happen. Only a small portion of these kinds of dreams ever come true., in fact, these dreams can prove harmful to us when we follow them with blind hope.

Jeremiah 23:16 This is what the Lord Almighty says:; " Do not listen to what the prophets are prophesying to you; they fill you with false hopes. They speak visions from their own minds,not from the mouth of the Lord. God's presence with us is a reality

His love surrounds us even in our deepest dream. Gentleness from the Father to his children is like soft summer rain falling on budding Roses.. His love knows no bounds and peace, joy, patience, faithfulness, kindness and gentleness are the fruits of the harvest he brings to us for nurturing and disbursing to all his children throughout our lifetime. Dear God, I pray that you will fill me with your gentleness to sprinkle on all lives I touch each day and by the end of that day I will be able to say that I made one human being a little wiser, happier, or better in some way this one day. Thank you Amen!

For our comfort,in the day of judgment it will be according to our faithfulness., not according to our usefulness, our sincerity, not our success, according to our uprightness of our hearts,not according to our opportunities. Some lives are quick to blossom in the spring, but others take their time. When it appears we are awaiting a late blooming promise from God, wait for it. God is faithful in his children and his promises he will surely bring to pass. The medical Journals are always reaching out to people to encourage them to go for a daily walk. Exercise is healthy for our mind, body, and spirit. While our walk strengthens our heart muscles there is benefit for our souls. Walking along with God as our companion will honor God's command he gives to us.

My dear readers, Walking blamelessly is what we are called to do. This may sound like a direct command- not a suggestion, but one that needs to be taken seriously as we walk through life.

> *Isaiah 2:5 Come, descendants of Jacob, Let us walk in the light of the Lord.*

When you walk you walk with God use a worship tape or just pray as you move along. God is with you. Enjoy the special time and healing you share with your creator and look forward to each day walking with God in spirit and health.

Everyone hurts sometime in their life. While some do not wound as deeply as others nevertheless, there is still a wound, which calls for gentleness, kindness, patience, faithfulness, peace, and most importantly love- for without these fruits of the spirit fragile emotions will shatter like a broken mirror, and cause unwanted depression, anger, guilt, and hopelessness to gain a foothold in your life and shackle you to their strongholds indefinitely. Emotions are fragile and we must handle all people with the same fruits with no individual preference. Philippians 4:5 Warns us Let your gentleness be evident to all. The lord is near. Feelings are everywhere so be gentle.

> *Could we with ink the ocean fill,*
> *and were the skies of parchment made,*
> *Were every stalk on earth a quill, and every man a scribe by trade,*
> *To write the love of God above*
> *would drain the ocean dry.*
> *nor could the scroll contain the whole,*
> *though stretched from sky to sky.*

By Frederick M. Lehman

Lord, I am ready for my next lesson in knowing our Fruits of the Spirit.

GOODNESS: FAITHFULNESS IS A BLESSING

As we approached South Carolina I noticed the clean crisp air. We had just traveled 1500 miles in serious snow, ice, and bitter cold, and now, we were finally here in the warmth of Winter . I could not believe it was this warm and I was actually removing all my heavy clothing, but I was thrilled by this beautiful climate. What would have made everything perfect would have been to be able to move into our home then, but unfortunately, nothing had been prepared by anyone so we had to seek shelter once again at a nearby Motel. I was so drained from the drive and all the dogs were restless as well. I just wanted to find food for my family, a hot shower and close my eyes

After a restless night with dogs going back and forth for walks around the motel area I hit slumber land. I would deal with all issues in the morning, which seemed to arrive to quickly. We ended up staying for two more days because papers had to be passed and our lawyers were not at all ready, our utilities were not turned on, and our moving van was lost. I did no feel blessed. I was angry and felt lost. I was most disappointed at the contractor,who sold our beautiful home from under us. We could have already been in a home, instead we were like nomads and that was not a good feeling at all.

I remember turning toward heaven and saying "really Lord, really" throwing my hands above my head In frustration. I could never understand how Almighty God would place me in this drama .and yet,, he never left me and watched over me with care. I don't understand why he put up with me all my life for I was troubled child.

Micah 7: 18. Who is another God like you, who pardons sins and forgives the transgression of the remnant of his inheritance? You do not stay angry forever but delight to show mercy.

You cannot stay angry with your people, for your love to be merciful. Once again, you will have compassion on us. You will tread our sins beneath your feet: you will throw them into the depths of the ocean!! You will bless us as you promised Jacob long ago. You will set your love upon us as you promised our Father Abraham. Amen. I realized God had us waiting for a reason. We had to trust Him with everything for we could not move forward without his opening of doors to pass us through. Standing and waiting on the Lord is difficult to control our patience, but when things become tangled and everything is in a frozen state there is simply no other choice to make except trusting in Him.

A main characteristic of God is his goodness. This golden attribute shines brightly lighting up a sad and crippled world as God's truth brings hope and promise to a stagnant civilization. To accomplish God's goodness is simply be humble, always live for others, and never seek one's advantage. Goodness consists not in the outward things we do, but in the inward person we are. So profound, so needed in this dusty world.. God's goodness showered on me that day and I walked into a new home, one I hoped would heal my aching soul and bring me peace. Sometimes you have to bite the bullet and we certainly did during the following weeks.

We moved in expecting our movers to show, but they did not arrive for several days along with extremely rude drivers, who didn't care a fig for our treasured possessions. They began unloading throwing everything into our garage with little care of the contents. Once again, I called on Almighty God to rectify this recklessness.. his answer was hold fast and remember who you are. Do not lose faith or your peace. This to will pass- and as quickly as they unloaded, they were gone and I had the delightful task of bringing things in, unpacking, and finding a place for everything.

As I unpacked, boxes I found many antiques broken-big

surprise-the way they unloaded our belongings, it was a wonder everything was not damaged. I felt the tears weld up in my eyes as I saw precious gifts ruined,scratched, or broken. We must remember to listen closely to God's voice when trouble rages around us. When the agonies of life crush us. God has not moved away from us. Often, we have moved away from him. We need to return to him in faith and call on him for his strength.

> *Psalm 37: 23-24 The Lord makes firm the steps od the one who delights in him; Though he may stumble, he will not fall, For the Lord upholds him with his hand*

> *Psalm 34:4 I sought the Lord,and he answered me; He delivered me from all my fears.*

> *Psalm 34;19 A righteous person may have many troubles, But the Lord delivers him from them all:*

> *John 14:1 Do not let your hearts be troubled. You believe in God; believe also in me.*

As I sat late at night wrapped up in a borrowed sleeping bag reading scripture, I knew God was with me and deeply believed there was nothing that we would encounter where God would not make it right. I slept well that night exhausted from all unpacking and disappointments we had endured the past week I never forgot to thank him for bringing us safely to our destination and was thankful to God we did not use the same movers to bring our Victorian furniture to South Carolina. Somehow, I had not contracted with the same company and I believe God's grace guided me in making that choice.

We had sold our Salem home and bought our new home enabling us to be free and not saddled down with any mortgage. This was a blessed gift from God's goodness to not have a mortgage premium to encounter monthly, but our financial status was not good. We had no employment and one thing after another began going wrong with our 10 month old home we purchased

A note of caution to readers: Never trust a Realtor that threatens to sue you if you change your mind before you pass papers. Note, they cannot do this as long as there is no present owner of the home you are purchasing. We were new with this state rule, which we found out was not Gospel so we signed contracts and bought two years of updates. Everything promised in our contract was not done and we wound up fixing everything needed with our own money seriously draining our surplus of savings.

I held a stellar record as well as certifications in administration, leadership, education and could not find a teaching position other than part-time substitute, which I accepted because we needed income. My husband faced the same employment issues and could not gain full-time employment. He too, had to settle for part-time work, low pay, and layoffs . There was one whole year we had to live entirely on our savings. Everywhere we turned we were faced with a mountain preventing us from moving forward. We began thinking perhaps, we should leave this area and build a home in Myrtle Beach. I even set interviews for open School Directorships and received an offer. To accept meant I had to be in that area by Fall. The next six months were crazy busy, but God's goodness shone through for no matter what we always were able to meet our monthly bills as well as any need we encountered that was not expected.

Oh, the wonderful love of God always there in every circumstance. a high tower where the righteous can run into and seek shelter. Our contractor worked day and night to finish our new home at the beach. We packed up our belongings once again hoping this time we were on the right path. God has a sense of humor. He allowed us to place our present home on sale, yet, he blocked our sale so that we could not sell our home. Although, we had many prospective couples not one made any offer to purchase our home. Even when we dropped our price way down not one offer was given. We had written a contingency clause into our contract which would return all deposits to us if we did not sell our home by the agreed date. We all but tried to give away our home to make a sale, but when God says no you have to step back, accept His decision, and know it is the best one.

This time I did not unpack our garage. I guess deep in my heart I believed we will move when God is ready and I did not want to have to pack everything again. God had work for me to do with ministry and till I was finished He was not letting me change direction. How great is our God. Once more, He released his goodness on us protecting hurried choices. God will always come in the last few minutes when you are making a life changing decision. His right hand of mercy lifts you bringing you to a new understanding to your footsteps forward.

I recall a story about a family we knew back North, who decided to take their family ministry to Russia. They were there only a few weeks and every single thing that could go wrong in ministry did. The area they chose to live had very few living options that were suitable or safe and .their girls could not gain entrance to over crowded schools. These missionaries started helping lost and broken souls on the streets, and went to hospitals offering their help to care for sick babies. Anywhere they could they would go when needed, but money they had depended on to pay for their room and board did not come as expected and soon their surplus was exhausted. Neither the wife or husband could obtain employment of any kind, and they were two months in rental obligations.

They decided that they had to return home before they had no money to buy tickets. They packed up, paid their debts, and headed to leave. On the way out, they checked their mail, and inside one of the envelopes was a check of substantial money to stay one year to work their ministry. The check was from an unknown donor.. They looked for another apt and found a lovely one across from the park. A private school called on their previous application with two openings for the girls, and both parents received offers for employment at the hospital they had given so many hours of their time. God's goodness- oh yeah !!! nothing but our God could accomplish all that. Does God come in the last hour- the last minute. I believe He does. I'm waiting for our turn next.

> *Philippians 4:6 do not be anxious about anything, but in every situation, by prayer and petition, with thanksgiving, present your requests to God.*

Blessed are all you Saints, O God and King, who have traveled over the tempestuous seas of this mortal life, and have made the harbor of peace and felicity. Watch over us who are still in our dangerous voyage, and remember such as he exposed to the rough storms of trouble and temptation. Frail is our vessel and the ocean is wide: but as in your mercy you have set our course. So steer the vessel of our life toward the everlasting shore of peace, and bring us at length to the quiet haven of our heart's desire, where you, O our God, are blessed, and live and reign for ever and ever.

Remember goodness is a Godly quality, one that will fill your deepest soul and give others a satisfied and comfortable station in their lives. To feel goodness in your heart is an incredible gift from God but to bestow goodness where ever you go is remarkable and infectious.

> *Each day every breath you take remember*
> *Do all the good you can*
> *By all the means you can*
> *In all the ways you can*
> *In all the places you can*
> *At all the times you can*
> *to all the people you can*
> *As long as you ever can.*

We can rejoice,when we run into our problems and trials, for we know that they help us develop endurance. And endurance develops our character, and character strengthens our confident hope of salvation God's goodness was evident in all I did. Slowly our ministry began to grow as more Southerners recognized who I was and our ministry mission. I began to speak in organizations and even church. There were still a lot of questions concerning our ministry, but at least I had a foot in the door and I was not stepping back. I began to write books, and under God's supervision and inspiration I wrote my Autobiography titled " Sometimes It Rains" Breaking Chains of Bondage", A Shatter of Innocence" and The Littlest Snowflake." In addition, I wrote music to accompany my books.

God's grace and goodness was all around me when I unexpectedly won the prestigious Academia Music Award for my recording of "Shattered" as best Christian Gospel category 2016. I was so amazed and felt blessed God had allowed me this great opportunity. I flew to California in April 2016 for a huge red carpet affair where I was presented with my award.. When I look at this beautiful cherry wood frame with my name and accomplishment engraved on it all I can do is look up and thank God. for His goodness.

I do not care to fly the friendly skies at all, but there have been several times I have had to. If I had my way, I would just drive everywhere and skip the plane trip. Unfortunately, there are certain ares one cannot go to quickly unless by air flight and California was one. Eight hours and two changes later I was in California here I come for the first time- and not what I had expected. Cold, rainy, and the hotel I was booked at was under construction repair- so there was noise of machinery over my room the whole time I stayed. I did make a host of new artist friends and could not get enough of my hotel's incredible cuisine. I guess there were some perks compensating for poor hotel accommodations. Feeling ungrateful, I had to thank God to let him know I did appreciate his goodness.

> *Dear God, Thank you that I am in Christ, where I don't have to fabricate my own life I am so grateful that here I have your righteousness that is based on my faith in you . AMEN*

Sometimes I wonder where or what my life would be without my magnificent Savior to love, guide, and protect my every moment, thought,or deed. There is not one who knows me like He does. From a rising of the sun to sleep at night- He covers me with his mighty arms always there to hear my prayers of thanks and need. He is my comfort, my support, my courage, and my protector of all trials I face each day. He opens doors and lights my path onward through fear, trouble, and pain. With Him I am complete- without His guidance I am lost and blind to all purpose and obligation before me.

After my two daughters left the world I did not want to acknowledge this horrific loss. I covered myself in a mask of denial and retribution- much like mummies in deep dark Egyptian tombs. I spoke no evil, I saw no evil, and I heard no evil. I blamed the times we lived in, a cruelty of society, an indifference of family, and most importantly, I was frozen in an era of cascading memories, which kept me handicapped to a past of false understanding- leaving me with little to no chance of recognizing crucial steps I needed to climb to embrace recovery and my essential survival.. No writer, poet or song could repair the torn threading of my fragile beating heart. No exquisite shimmering jewel sparkling with radiance of sun and moonlight could capture the smiles I had lost forever in my world of reality. Time no longer existed in this world for me as I slept days, walked floors at night, and sometimes food was not even considered as I reached and grabbed a cookie or a bag of chips for a meal.

> *Samuel 2:6 tells us The lord brings death and makes alive; He brings down to the grave and raises up, funny how we forget so easily the magnitude of Almighty God. He is all we need.*

SELF CONTROL: PATIENCE

So many of us have lost the battle, and then ultimately, the war. A direct result of losing self control of words and, actions to others. How many battered women wind up as victims- then fatalities, because of the other partner's lack of self control. Each year, approximately four million American women alone are abused by their partners-resulting in three deaths a day- Ten percent of these women's battle are recurring and regular. This travesty in just our America can be blamed on alcohol, personality, money, family wars, divorce, mental disorders, or drugs- but this all boils down to lack of self-control of emotions, words,, and actions. Every day the media are broadcasting someone is shot, school children are attacked, and people are missing simply summed up to lack of self control of the perpetrator.

Self- control is an integral foundation of the fruits of the spirit. Did you ever wonder how wonderful this world could be if there were no objection to rules and regulations of society? There would be no contempt of court, because everyone being tried would have self control in having their turn. There would be no breaking a restraining order because self control of wanting to would lose to self governing of one's actions.

Everyone carries on an inward talk with themselves; those who have learned not to answer back in anger,knowing that the one who conquers himself is braver than the one who conquers his enemies. Self- control is made up of so many attributes. There is strength in self-control which reveals a strong character.

Isaiah 40 28-31

Do you not know?
Have you not heard?
The Lord is the everlasting God,
The Creator of the ends of the earth.
He will not grow tired or weary,
and his understanding no one can fathom.
He gives strength to the weary
and increases the power of the weak.
Even youths grow tired and weary,
And young men stumble and fall;
but those who hope in the Lord
will renew their strength.
They will soar on wings like eagles.
They will run and not grow weary.
They will walk and not be faint.

I remember back when I was about to be interviewed for a top Administrative position at a large Children's facility. As I sat waiting to be called I looked at the perspective students all eager to land this position. Why not? Excellent pay, schedule, and benefits. The position was Director of the Early Childhood Program. I was a bundle of nerves all morning and thought can I do this? I will never meet their specifications.

My thoughts raced through my mind blocking everything out that made sense. My hands shook and I was sure I was going to forget my delivery, and kept peeking at my notes to review my message. In the midst of my terror, I .never denied who I was and God made me this way. God gave me this opportunity knowing this moment would come. I stepped forward in my weakness— and Al mighty God met me there. He was there with my pounding heart, shaky voice, and trembling hands. After the interview, my co-workers were shocked to know I was so traumatized . It made me think. Suppose I had denied my weakness- would God have denied me as well? Even the most paralyzing fear cannot interfere with his great power and strength. He had walked me through a time I had no faith in myself and revealed to me a strong purposeful woman of God.

Thank you Jesus for your mercy and grace. May I always hold your hand through my worst fears and doubt. May you always pick me up and set my feet solid on the ground, and may I know without any doubt I can do all things in your name .Amen!! God's wonderful strength to face strongholds, pressure, and disappointment is a foundation of self control. In addition to strength, there is a great need for patience. Patient people can use rationale for their problems, logic, wisdom, and discernment.There is a wealth of strength in patience, and patience brings you to the doorway of peace.

> *John 14:27 " Peace I leave with you. My peace I give you. I do not give to you, as the world gives do not let your heart be troubled and do not be afraid." Those words were spoken by Jesus. It can't be better. The bible teaches t us to pursue righteousness, godliness, faith, love, endurance, and gentleness: To Fight the good fight..*

Self-Control is in fact an attribute of great strength – a forever fruit of the spirit ready for picking at Harvest time. The Lord is with you when you are with him. If you seek him, he will be found by you

> *Chronicles 15:2 Let us then approach the throne of grace with confidence, so that we may receivemercy and find grace to help us in our time of need..*

> *Psalm 55:22 is a promise for us from God.. Cast your cares on the Lord and he will sustain you. The Lord is our friend. He enjoys walking with us as our companion on life's pathway, and he brings blessing into our lives when we walk closely with him.*

Dearest Lord (my prayer)

Thank you for caring for me and guiding my path
Each day I am thankful for another chance to serve you
Your sun so bright through my window captures my attention
when I walk outside I am surrounded by its warmth
you perfume my space with sweet odors of flowers
when it rains I know you will set a rainbow, a promise of love
You watch over me as I sleep and calm my soul
I am aware of the power of your name
I believe you have tasks I must honor to bring glory to you
but you must direct my path for me to walk in victory
You have been there through all my trials throughout the years
although I have been shattered
You, God, have never abandoned me. Amen

By Your Faithful Servant Joan

When you possess the amazing love of God and you walk in His ways, when you exhibit each fruit if His harvest- you are blessed and are in season to his faith. Learning lessons has brought me to a new and crucial understanding of how God works in each of us irregardless of our circumstances, or where we are in life. Perhaps,the most incredible moment for us in God's garden of fruit is in recognition of the combination to a fruitful life. A harvest of the heart living a fruitful life means living with knowledge there is something more important than our own life.

Part Two: Trials

Loss Unimaginable

Grief Unbearable

Loss to most can be categorized as losing a job, home, or security. Loss may also refer to a vehicle or possession held sacred,/personal. Perhaps, the most meaningful loss of life relative to family or friend would be considered tragic for a person /family to experience. All these losses are within framework of expected losses experienced during their lifetime. All of the above losses indicated can be rectified by insurance and other financial appropriations for recovery. One exception to this list, which is never resolved is loss of a life and when loss is a close relative such as a daughter, son, mother, father, or spouse-loss becomes profound irregardless of circumstances

We try to create excuses excepted by society as perfectly acceptable as to why we do not attend a social event, or complete a minor shopping obligation. We shut the doors and windows of our present and spend valuable moments looking back. Never look back!!!! Looking back brings you to a depressed status of regrets, indecision, depression, and guilt. We often refer to hindsight being 20/20, but in essence, when we return to crossroads of wishing we could change the past, we fail to consider consequence more painful than joyful. These times you need a fresh supply of fruit delicately applied to your spirit with God's wisdom spiraling you forward. God has delivered us from such a deadly peril, and he will deliver us. On Him we have set our hope that he will continue to deliver us.

Dear God- Thank you for being my world, my peace, my joy, my all. Thank you for being my wisdom, and my strength for without you, I would be a failure stuck in my world of regret. You have brought me to a new understanding and I am both grateful and blessed you love me, watch over me, and carry me when I cannot walk on my own . Amen.

Many things that God might ask from us could go against our nature, but I urge you to walk it out with God on a consistent basis by faith, even when it becomes most difficult. My children were the deepest loss I have ever endured. In my deepest sorrow as darkness of my existence flashed across the skies painting scenes of my loss- I stretched my hands out to God in deep anguish. The Lord met me where I was, dried my tears, lifted my soul from my pit of darkness, and held my hand each time I stumbled to regain my composure.

> *Psalm 84:11- 12 The Lord God is a sun and shield: The Lord bestows favor and honor: no good thing does he withhold from those whose walk is blameless. O Lord Almighty, blessed is the man who trusts in you.*

Magnificent Savior. Even when you don't feel his presence he is behind the scenes still working for those who love him and are called according to his purpose.

> *Isaiah 41;10 So do not fear for I am with you: do not be dismayed, for I am your God. I will strengthen you and help you: I will uphold you with my righteous hand.*

I am quite sure that my loss was not as nearly traumatic as God's when He gave his one and only son to the world to set us free, and He was beaten, humiliated, and nailed to the cross. Jesus died for our freedom. He laid down his life so that we would not have to pay any cost for our sins. He took it all. What greater love than this to lay down your life for another. The loss I felt could never compare to that and yet, God and I share a common bond in loss. No matter what- loss is a tremendous void in your life; one where you look to the heavens and ask why? When we look back over our lives with regrets and if only, we rob ourselves of hope and the joy of God's grace

When we do look back, we must do so with God's perspective. Then we can trace His hand on our lives, and see that He has transformed the bad into good, just as He promised he would. God's promises are true and because we know that as a given there is not any rationale you can accommodate to the answer faith brings us when we as believers walk the walk and talk the talk in faith and truth.

Dear God- when I am lost and seeking refuge I remember my safe place I can go to for comfort.

Psalm 121:1-8

I lift up my eyes to the mountains--
Where does my help come from?

My help comes from the Lord,
The maker of heaven and earth

He will not let your feet slip---
He who watches over you will not slumber:

Indeed, he who watches over Israel will neither slumber nor sleep.
The Lord watches over you--

The Lord is your shade of your right hand:;
The sun will not harm you by day,,

Nor the moon by night.
The Lord will keep you from all harm--

He will watch over your life;
The Lord will watch over your coming and going

Both now and forevermore. Amen!
Scripture after scripture- Psalm after psalm tells the
incredible majestic status of our Lord God Almighty.

Revelation 4:8

Holy, holy, holy
is the Lord God Almighty,
who was, and is, and is to come

God- you are my shield, my helper, my fortress, my deliverer, my strength, my refuge. You are my glorious sword, my eternal protection, my loving God. You are the Horne of my salvation, the rock in whom I take refuge,the one who gives glory, and lifts my head. My heart trusts in you and leaps for joy! You are a God who does not grow tired or weary, whose unlimited patience endures,whose compassion never fails. Great is your faithfulness.

Life is not a all Roses and God never promised us a flower garden. Our path is in front of us and up to each one to make their choice which way to walk. Though we stumble – we get back up- though we are blind- we begin to see. God is always at a distance watching us and we are never left to face our trials in darkness. There is nothing to small or to large for God to handle. We can do all things through our God who strengthens us. As I learned lessons every day in my time spent with God and\His word I began to understand events of my lifetime that seemed strange and confusing to me at one time,yet suddenly the dark was lighter and my burden lifted..

We can never forget our loss especially, when we are in a state of depression compounded by earth shattering trials. Sorrow can cause us to doubt Gods plan. Though we may face trouble and difficulties, sadness and pain, God is still in control, and He is always with us. The very first and most important principle we need to realize is

God is in control. This is a large block to our healing because we cannot- or will not let go. God simply does not step in to our picture when we have a do not enter sign posted. First, this clearly informs Him we are not ready to listen. Last, we need to understand when loneliness overtakes us and we need to return to Him in faith. God has promised to always be with us and that is our bottom line to consider in our healing process.

He will never forsake us. Lean on his promises and receive his peace, which is one of our attributes in fruits of the spirit. When agonies of life crush us, we must remember that our God has not moved away from us. We have moved away from him. We need to return to Him in faith and call on Him for His strength. I sought the Lord and he answered me: He delivered me from all my fears. Psalm: 34-4. I always remember this prayer. Of mine every morning .

Dear God when I awake please start my day with
your covering of safety and love with
Christ before me, Christ within me
Christ behind me, Christ before me
Christ beside me, Christ to comfort and restore me,
Christ beneath me,Christ above me
(A quote by Saint Patrick)

Amen!

In loss we recognize there is no turning around and everything will be corrected. Our state of loss is permanent and never forgotten. Our only way to manage our sorrow is through acceptance. When we face loss, or pain, we take comfort knowing that no trial is too deep for Almighty God to set us free from all burden. He desires to instill within us His divine comfort.

Matthew 11: 28-29 "come to me, all you who are weary and
burdened, and I will give you rest Take my yoke upon you and

learn from me, for I am gentle and humble in heart, and you will find rest for your souls."

Though things may seem hopeless at times, God who has called you into fellowship with his son Jesus- Christ our Lord is faithful. No pain is so great that he does not bring us comfort.

As I write about loss, it seems almost parallel that at present we are facing historical hurricane, Florence. I stop to think about repercussions that will develop from this brutal attack of nature. At 1:30 in the afternoon 175 winds in miles per hour approaching South Carolina this dangerous category 4 storm will hit hard our peaceful Carolina. Both North and South Carolina will sustain enormous loss, not only homes, personal property, utilities, automobiles, personal items, but more importantly, loss of lives among people and animals. As we do not have a Noah or a Noah's Ark to save us from torrential rains and flooding, we turn to God for He alone is our refuge and protector from danger.

As millions all over the world stop this week to remember 9/11- that fated day, when terrorists attacked United States with airplanes resulting in loss of life that was catastrophic in number. .Does anyone ever really know when the bell will toll? We don't ask why? It's not for us to answer. As Jews all over the world come together to bring in the Jewish New Year with atonement, blowing of the Ram's horn initiating repentance to God, and seeking another year ending without loss. In these turbulent times we turn to God who knows each ending. As scripture tells us

Revelation 22;13 " I am the Alpha and the Omega, the First and the Last, the Beginning and the End".

If I could have known what would happen in my life, or how much loss I would endure in a lifetime, I would have to be truthful in answering I wish that those losses never happened, but we are given free choice to walk our paths as we choose, and God will only interfere when we ask Him to. He wants us to act with our hearts and not out of necessity. Some losses can be explained while others cannot. We have to incorporate all our logic to truly understand that sometimes losses cannot be changed and there is nothing we can do to change circumstances. It is what it is so- let the river run. Simply stated, don't fight a losing battle and always remember He loves us and that alone is our save.

"I praise you O Lord, for the incredible value you place on sinners. You do not passively wait for us to come to you. You actively, passionately seek us out of our wondering and hiding places. Your pursuit is relentless. Nine out of ten is not acceptable for you. Ninety -nine out of one hundred is still not good enough for you. You are not willing that any should perish. You desire all people to repent, be saved, and to come to the knowledge of truth. When you find us you carry us on your shoulders into safety of the fold. You rejoice over us with saints and angels

> *"Thank you Lord for your limitless, bountiful, passionate, merciful, fervent, never ending love".*

God is close to the brokenhearted. When you experience loss of a loved one God is right there walking through your pain along side of you. When you feel you cannot make it through your heartache, God will carry you in his loving arms. Remember- what God brings us to – He will see us through. Our trials will never consume us.

> *Lamentations 3:22-23 Because of the Lord's great love we are not consumed, for his compassion never fails. They are new every morning; great is your faithfulness.*

"Dear Lord, will you never cease your kindly care over us, and may we also continue unceasingly to bless you for all your past and present blessings in Jesus:name." Amen!! Yesterday is gone, tomorrow may never come- we have today to be all God has called us to. "O most loving Savior, in the light of this new day may the sunshine of your presence shine upon our souls. Dispel the darkness from our minds and wills: teach us how to walk and what to do. We thank you for the opportunity of duties and responsibilities before us .give us willing hearts that we may patiently and faithfully toil this blessed day so that at its close, we can say truly, this was one more day's work for you in your trial.

When you are faced with bewildering circumstances we may be tempted to ask why?.A better question to seek an answer from the Lord is asking what? What do you have in mind now Lord?

He tells us in *Jeremiah 33:3 "Call to me and I will answer you and tell you great and unsearchable things you do not know.*

Though it may seem that things are out of control, we can take comfort in God's enduring promises and constant presence. O sheltering Almighty God. Shadows may gather round me, as on my journey I go. Yet they can never confound me, sunshine will come soon, I know. Push away all doubt. Cast out all confusion. Stand firm in the Lord and find a renewed faith following in His footsteps. The word loss is a most profound explanation to capture a cause for grief.. Webster dictionary tells us that "grief is the pain of mind, resulting from loss, misfortune,injury, or evils of any kind; sorrow; regret." Grief enters our life at some point however, grief has different levels of the severity and variety of an experience relevant to our loss.

Lessons we encounter and digest are for immediate application not for us to transfer them to a back burner for future application. What good would these lessons be and where would our discernment fall if we did not take to heart our trials and our lessons learned? Simply stated, where would our victory be if we did not use the mind of Christ when we come faced with overwhelming circumstances?

Romans 8: 35 who shall separate us from the love of Christ?

Does this mean He no longer cares for us when we bring Him trouble, calamity, persecution, or we are hungry or destitute threatened with death. The answer to this is no!! Despite all these conditions, we have still victory through Christ, who loved us. When we are experiencing infinite loss, we do not acknowledge even the smallest victory in our lives because we are not able to grasp the fullness of God's love for us and dismiss any possible probability of healing our tormented souls. We are as homeless as the barefoot wanderer when we walk away from God's protection.

Majority speaks loudly and boldly over rationale. Thinking in terms of logic- all reason is gone and anger, denial, and depression remain your guardians. In my own great loss, I was not humble, thankful, or faithful. I wanted to be inside a bubble where nothing and nobody could reach me. What was once a loving heart became an empty shell of bitterness and loneliness. Reality had ceased to exist and hope had fled from my body and soul. I found myself in search of all the why questions instead of turning to God and asking Him what was next for me to do? I wanted a miracle to occur right at the moment I felt loss. Miracles do not have to break natural law to become a supernatural event.

When Christ stilled the storm, he didn't set aside universal law-the storm would have eventually subsided on its own: instead, He directed the weather pattern. When Elijah prayed for it to stop raining, God directed the natural drought and rain. When you thrust yourself in the main waters of of God's world plan, and pray God please use me!!! Miracles arrive along with angels, resources, and all people needed for your ministry. Jabez- believed the hand of God was necessary to be touching him for success in whatever plan he undertook. The phenomenal success of the early church was largely credited to only one reason, which was the hand of God was with them. This belief brought many to turn to the Lord. The hand of God soon was replaced by the filling of the spirit. We are so blessed to be filled with this spirit and yet, we only acknowledge this incredible strength when we feel there is no other means to our dilemma. Almighty God did not want us to ignore this great gift – in fact, God desires for us to use His holy spirit every day of our lifetime. Sometimes, when we are caught up in chaos, there is no time to use rational thinking, and so we struggle to survive our loss with no direction before us, or any hope for a future. God will never ever leave us in our time of sorrow. Our loss may seem an enormous burden but take heart, it is never to much for God to shoulder. God's words ring true and clear"

> Isaiah 43:2 *When you pass through the waters, I will be with you: and when you pass through the rivers, they will not sweep over you. When you walk through the fire, you will not be burned; the flames will not set you ablaze.*

At this point, I ask the reader how do you feel when someone offers compassion to you when you are struggling? In addition, what does it mean to you when God cares deeply for your burden and wants to carry you through it all? Are we comforted or are we so grief stricken we cannot accept any of God's mercy or His people's love. If those questions cannot be answered with a positive note, then you have crossed the imaginary line we know as grief, which we will discuss in depth for the next part of our bondage in pain.

There is a time for our mending broken hearts, crushed dreams, and forgotten bridges. We never know or understand rationale for our steps when we enter a destructive and horrific event which is our very foundation- yet, what remains is always a way home through faith and acknowledgment that we are one of many pebbles in a not so perfect world where evil reigns and good fights evil every second we breathe. There is never a way back only forward to new paths of light, joy, and peace. A new time of harvest and revelation.

When I lost my daughters, I never believed I would ever laugh again. Throw in the towel and what did it matter for without my children in my life where was my joy? Locked up in cruel circumstances and sadness I lost many days and hours of my life. Time marched on but I could not. I had no schedule and broke appointments, which for me was against my nature. I was always organized, punctual, and eager to meet my responsibilities both professionally and personally. That was all before my loss- very different perspective toward life after grief set in and claimed me.

Our help will always come from God.l always come from the Lord. He is the only one who can quiet the rage within us. Knowing this I called out to the Lord and He heard me. Sing praises to the Lord for Heis our fortress, our strength, and our hope. Loss is lonely when you are within confines of this pain by yourself, and I chose to stay alone regardless of well wishes, family, neighbors, and friends,who tried to minister to my great need. Where was this love of God? Love was all around me but my deep withdrawal from reality blinded me to all outreached arms and healing words of comfort.

Proverbs 25:20

Like one who takes away a garment on a cold day,
Or like vinegar poured on a wound
Is one,who sings songs to a heavy heart.

When the outlook is not good we should not fret. We need a change of perspective to recognize that God sees tomorrow more clearly than we see yesterday. Our future is entirely in his hands.

GRIEF

When we enter into grief we pass through hallways, loss, and begin to encounter reasons we need to understand to our healing process. Time is not a pleasant addition to our nemesis, but more of a gradual numbness within our bodies and mind. Still without explanation- still without rest- we seek our way moving toward a solution that brings us justice for all involved. In my case, there were many near and dear participants, who played both major and minor roles resulting in my unspeakable loss, and yet, this all was meaningless for as Ecclesiastes says There is a time to be born- and there is a time to die. There was not one person who could be charged for this loss. God grants us all freedom of choice and when we choose to enter a deadly path of no return- then we can expect a horrendous ending.

Matthew 6:13 warns us " And do not lead us into temptation,
but deliver us from evil"

Nothing is indicated about special powers, or spiritual insight. There is nothing said about confrontation for that model prayer. How many times did I remember to ask for safekeeping for my daughters, and did they ever ask for safe boundaries on their own lives? The first question involves me and yes, I pleaded for my daughters on my knees, but they still had final say on their destructive voyages. I had no power and God had been shunned. When circumstances such as these spiral there is almost a devastating result that will enter in and sweep all peace, humility, joy, goodness, mercy, and most importantly love into a burning pit of ashes.

Their mistake was not in hanging on a precipice,but in being there without Almighty God watching and protecting them from falling into the fiery abyss- directly delivered to waiting hands of the deceiver. God deeply desires us to reach out to Him.

Dear God, Protect me from all pain and grief that has entered my life. Because of my pride and carelessness I may be in danger and so I implore you to please place a supernatural boundary surrounding me with your precious power. Thank you Father. Amen!

Our grief deposits us right at the foot of satan. We must walk through this tortuous valley of death and because God assures us He will never leave us- we have to move in blind faith that Hr is walking beside us each step we put forth. Psalm 23:4 clearly emphasizes our position- even though I walk through the shadow of death, I will fear no evil. For you are with me, thy rod and thy staff they comfort me. His promise of never leaving our side regardless of circumstance is an engraved contract correlating God's promise to his people. Even when our world is going crazy wrong- He will still be with us. Grief is intolerable, bruising, stifling,shameful, mocking, and tears your insides to pieces.

You cannot hide, deceive, or deny heart wrenching grief. There is no escape, and no excuse. Grief claims you and you are shackled without God to release your burden. When we understand that anger, denial, and guilt do not serve as a release of our burden we can begin to focus on things that will bring us toward a path of restoration and purpose for our lives. What is the final outcome when we wade through every muddy foothold of reality and know for certain that we are not in any manner equipped to ask why?

His answers may not be what we hoped for or they might be only partial explanation to quiet our badly bruised soul. God delights in those who trust in him. He is Almighty God who knows all and loves unconditionally. As Christians, we have to come to a realization that He is the only one to know the fullness of a loss. His timing is perfect and His planned design for all those who are righteous knows no boundaries.This all is according to precision of time. I am more than content knowing Lauren and Melanie received their answers to all questions asked by them.

To continue grieving asking why and if only draws us into bitterness and misery which are burdens a loving God does not desire for us to be dragged down. God is not just keeper of all answers – He is our infinite and eternal deliverance from loss and grief. Although, my girls are not here on special holidays or events around family, I know with deep certainty that they are temporarily absent from our lives, but never forgotten. I understand that they are with God and there is no safer place for them to be until we meet again and dance on streets of gold together praising and worshiping our Savior. My separation from my daughters is only a brief moment in time. What follows is eternal togetherness- a reconciliation of abounding love, and unspeakable joy. When I look through eyes of faith I see Melanie and Lauren as they were not in their last years of struggling to live, but with a view of two loving sisters frolicking on our living-room floor, or riding their bikes intensely trying to beat their deadline hungry for their evening meal.

To understand this somehow brings me perfect peace, one that can only come from God's mighty hand on our broken lives. To understand this will somehow repair the torn side of our bodies where grief entered in to reside. One of the most profound thinkers our country was fortunate to call our brother was Benjamin Franklin.

This great thinker believed that "A man is not completely born until he is dead" Franklin viewed our existence as an embryonic state as we were in our Mother's womb. He further believed that this was a preparatory class of learning for true living.

Our bodies are lent to us for purpose of serving Almighty God. When our bodies become riddled down with illness and sin and we no longer can serve God in his plan for us- then that is the time when

He ends our torment and takes us home. The real question is why should we spend valuable time grieving when God will at his appointed time take us also. As long as we know where our loved ones are we will find them and rejoice. That promise of God is more than enough to set our feet back firm on level ground and move forward to a new pathway. At the very moment you call out to God for relief from your devastation- He rescues you and surrounds you with his feathers of comfort and protection. Darkness begins to lift and there is a sudden clarity of your grief you never knew existed before- one which brings you forward to a new venue filled with peace of what your next step is in your unending search for understanding.

God is the only one who can move our mountains of grief, guilt, despair, loneliness, and loss. I have found and believe firmly that the battlefield of all mentioned above belongs to the Lord. He is equipped for these wars against humanity and simply stated, we are not. Psalm 40:5 recalls His glory to mind. Many, O Lord my God, are the wonders you have done. The things you planned for us no one can recount to you: were I to speak and tell of them, they would be too many to declare. You are the one who says " I am the Lord, your God, who takes hold of your right hand and says to you, do not fear; I will help you. Thank you, Lord my God, for showing the wonder of your great love by saving me so many instances in my lifetime.

> *Dear God, every day I face a myriad of decisions – some major – some trivial. Please help me to make wise choices and select the right path. Your word tells us all we have to do is ask, and here I am asking for your grace and mercy on my trials facing me.*

*Thank you for your compassion and more importantly your
love.*

*Your faithful Servant Joan
There is none like you
No one can touch my heart the way that you do,
I could search the earth my whole life through
There would be no one like you*

By Michael W. Smith

All I can say here is Amen!

When I begin to look at the whole picture I saw truth as I had never known before. Denial of losing my daughters kept me bound in a cage of guilt and sadness in which I could not free myself from this daily burden heavily ingrained upon my soul. Is it well within my soul. I can honestly reply at that moment – it was not!!. Looking at finality knowing I could not flip a page of circumstances backward to change facts bluntly staring me in my face was certainly the hardest and longest period of my lifetime. Would searing pain never reach an end? Looking through eyes of faith was my only save- but at that time depression was my only friend. In my darkness I questioned existence of God. Well wishes from others meant nothing for me, and days and nights became a blur of memories flooding my exhausted mind.. Rationale had no plausible explanation for my grief and I was lost in a time of no return.

Sometimes it is impossible for me to rest because I have never been shown how. I am not familiar with being at rest in the hollow of your hand, nor am I even vaguely aware I can find peace under your protection. I have always been considered a take charge person – to never lay back any part of my control. That was my strength yet. not at anytime, was I taught to relax. Therefore, I never was privy to role models, which served as examples to follow. Jesus, when you walked through Jerusalem and its hills, you pioneered this way of living. You were alert and submissive to the will of the Father. Multitudes of demands were placed on you and yet, you worked in perfect peace and power.

> *My prayer is help me walk in your steps. Teach me to have your vision, and to say what you say. Please help me Lord to work resting and to pray resting I ask this all in your mighty name. Thank you. Amen.*

If our grief could turn us to soaking prayer when all seems lost we would find there is a special joy that we receive when we come face to face with our Savior. His presence alone in prayer fills us with exuberant joy. We experience this joy in prayer because of our partnership in prayer. We experience joy in prayer because of answers to prayer. We receive joy in prayer because it is a place of repentance. The reason joy so vital to our existence is first, joy is an essential element and a necessary characteristic of God's kingdom. Secondly, Joy is the fruit of the Spirit, and lastly "the joy of our Lord is our strength"

Grief is time consuming soaking up all our energy, health, and hope. Where does each day end or begin for everything appears on a revolving turn table of time and space. Nothing matters for you only want to get through the next minute without falling into oblivion. Escaping grief is not an option or choice. Simply stated, grief is a way of life and no matter how we try to avoid grief there is no escape. As the teacher in Ecclesiastes mentions continuously everything under the sun is meaningless. When we are grieving we enter a state of meaningless where nothing makes sense to our life and yet, we can rejoice too when we run into problems and trials for we know they help us develop endurance.

> *Psalm 32:7*
> *You are my hiding place;*
> *you will protect me from trouble*
> *and surround me with songs of deliverance.*

Everyone applies different methods to move them through their loss and sadness. Some use enormous amounts of sleep to hide from their sorrow. Some use alcohol to numb their pain, and others use drugs of various means to stabilize their life. None of these hideouts work and when they are at a low degree of medicating your body and mind into a state of feeling nothing you awake with things even worse than they appeared before- because this is reality and reality is cruel and hopeless. I was one of th blessed ones because I had God back in my life and my music to praise and worship Him throughout lonely days.

Blessed art you O' Lord our king, who have traveled over tempestuous seas of mortal life,and have made the harbor of peace and felicity.. Watch over us, who are still in our dangerous voyage; and remember being exposed to rough storms of life with its trouble and temptations.. Frail is our vessel, and the ocean is wide .In your mercy precious Lord- you have set our course. Please steer our vessel of life toward the everlasting shores of peace, and bring us at length to a quiet haven of our heart's desire - where you, O our God are blessed, and reign for ever and ever Amen.

When we grieve we must realize that although, we have no hope- we have today to pray for this moment. Now into God's arms I pray for

Today's tasks, failures, and obstacles before me. I pray for forgotten memories and to always remember those, who were in my life .I pray for clarity in judgment, victories in areas I touch, and always to support unconditional love for all. I pray for sweet blessings and growth in my ministry, and an increase in my territory. I bless all the lost sheep especially, those,who do not know you. I ask today,if it be your will. for restoration and hope to flow in abundance, and more importantly, I ask for peace, joy, and love as I lead the lost. Thank you Lord for your compassion, strength,grace,and wisdom. Amen

Psalm 117:2 For great is his love toward us, and the faithfulness of the Lord endures forever.

My grief was channeled like a roller coaster. The only difference was in reality a roller coaster will stop at the end of a ride and release its hostages. In grief, my roller coaster experience never ended, nor released the bondage of sadness and pain I felt throughout every day. In the few brief minutes I seemed to be grounded I would acknowledge God' s love and compassion- a profound joy to compensate my times of relentless grief. There were multiple valleys where grief over ruled my peace of mind and my music was a gift during those blinding moments of indecision and regret. I began to reflect on scriptures that brought me to new understanding and doors of possibilities. In the eleventh chapter of John's Gospel John recorded the words of Jesus. *"I am the resurrection and the life" Those who believe in me even though they die like everyone else. will live again." John 11:25.*

I knew both my daughters had believed in Christ and honored their Savior. Melanie had been first to become a Christian and Lauren, a late bloomer did fully encompass the truth of God before she died. I know with certainty they are alive- not dead, and share in God's perfect promise of everlasting life. There is no stone that will not turn or a leaf that will not fall without God's mighty hand .Like the new born babe unwrapped from his Mother's womb, God had unwrapped my two daughters from their pain and earthly suffering. They now are in the holy presence of God Almighty in praise, worship, and joy in the Lord.

If there are no substantiated patterns to measure grief- and grief is unpredictable- and even illogical, then how can we create the perfect model to grieve? First, I would suggest and support you to recognize and not deny your grief. Yes, my heart is bruised and bleeds but I have learned that denial is a hostile and damaging state to practice. In addition, I carry all my burdens and lay them down at the foot of His throne and walk away. He heals my heart and assures me my daughters are with Him and they are well. Lastly, There is a release when you openly acknowledge your sorrow and open up yourself to new beginnings. This allows your wounds to knit together and become less of a nemesis to your continual process of healing.

In essence, No person's grief is greater than another, and- no time extended is determined as a rule. Although, you believe you are alone in this process- you are not. Almighty God will walk along beside you guiding your every step into an unfamiliar territory of new beginnings regardless of time or intensity. Whether we find ourselves questioning God's reason for allowing certain things to happen, we must stop,remember God's faithfulness, and depend upon His grace. Whatever our circumstances- God is still in control. And he will fulfill his purpose for my life.

Part Three: Steps

Revelation: Facing the Truth

Unification, and clarity of Fruits of the spirit from lessons learned and comprehension of our experiences through trials, shifts us to a new trajectory of moving upward and forward into revelation of our problem. When we become blinded by doubt and denial there is no opportunity for our minds to walk on our journey of rationale. As I thought about happy times with Melanie, I recalled one precious time We were planning a Thanksgiving meal together. We had been preparing all day and by the time we were at the point of finalizing our purchasing a Turkey to complete our shopping schedule for that day, Melanie and I were exhausted. Of course, when you enter a state of exhaustion everything you see or do appears funny.

Melanie had left my vision to look at another area where Turkeys were larger. I had just selected a good size bird when I heard Melanie laughing. She had an infectious laugh so no one could ever make an error identifying her. I looked up to see my adult daughter sitting on a turkey and hopping toward me as if she were on a bouncy ball. I was shocked but could not help laughing at this scene. " Come and try this Mom. It is so much fun" I looked at the turkey in my arms and thought- why not- never thinking I should not be doing this. Soon Melanie and I were hopping from aisle to aisle on turkeys with one irate manager chasing us through the store. Melanie and I ditched our turkeys and ran from the store almost hysterical. We had to go buy our turkey somewhere else that day, but our experience was one I never forgot.

Both Melanie and Lauren were my warriors if someone ever attacked me. They would approach the offender right in their face defending me furiously. I was blessed that they both shared this protective feeling toward their Mom and never left me alone to answer to insult. Melanie and Lauren had special gifts of spirit and laughter that would lift others no matter what trials they were experiencing, Between heavy trials, accomplishments, and dreams- Melanie and Lauren left us a life insurance policy that we will see them again. This is one insurance policy I don't have to pay any monthly or yearly premium to enforce. God provides that protection in scripture over and over. An authentic truth of God's mercy and grace to those,who have suffered loss assures us a reunion unlike any we have ever experienced in this lifetime.

Is there any way one can prepare for grief?. Absolutely yes- if you are faithful in living with your commitment to Christ. There comes a not expected revelation that you can deal effectively with anything if you recognize Christ as Lord. This complete understanding assures you your final home is with Him and with that certainty, you have removed a major concern from your mind of mixed emotions. As you walk through your valley of sadness, you will view it as springs where prayers and blessings refresh your battered soul after the pouring rains of pain. During my period of revelation. I began to focus on every unleashed memory that triggered my soul's sadness.

After I lost my daughters, questions arose in my mind. These questions helped me enormously as I began to turn my focus to things other than my loss with constant pain I experienced, My revelation began to mount as I thought of multiple factors relating to my sadness which was now worthy of my focus. I call these revelations listed below my principles to recovery.

First and foremost I carried no fear regarding where my loved ones were. I knew with certainty they were home with the Lord and no longer experienced pain or sadness.. They were whole, alive, and vibrant basking in all that eternal life brought before them.

My second positive revelation was I had always loved my daughters with all my heart and never turned away when going became rough and tough love was needed. My daughters knew that I loved them every moment even when love was all that I had left to give them. This important necessary aspect- not having to apologize with " if only" was a burden that I no longer carried as I began to move forward to healing.

My third revelation focused on one fact- which was I had perfect peace in God's plan. There was never doubt or fear within my belief that changed my faith in God. When I first experienced my loss, I was angry, tortured, resentful,and hopeless. Under God's mighty hand and gentle mercy I learned my lessons well and found error in my thinking was the main reason I was not healing. Revelation of God's timing revealed a new day for my two daughters and knowing they were safe from all evil filled my soul with wellness and joy.

My final revelation revealed a loving God not one that was cruel in taking my girls in fact, was merciful. Both Melanie and Lauren suffered with wrong choices both in their relationships and wellness facets. God saw their desperate need to come home and He allowed this because of His great love for them. When I acknowledged this fact, rationale returned. I saw clearly truth of their death, and how incredible merciful God is to His children. All I could think at my moment of truth was what an amazing God we serve. And now my tears are filled with gratefulness to a God,who saw beyond our pain and carried us not only to it -but through it.

Composers Bill and Gloria Gaither wrote this song

> *Because He lives – I can face tomorrow- and that says it all dear reader. All my positives reflected a loving God and thanks and glory to Him who sits on the throne. To live in a way that wins others to Christ expresses love of Christ. In this way we will assure and love others.*

Dear God, I will try to do my best to live in a state of forgiveness, love, and faith. I know this pattern will be excellent preparation for grief in my future. To follow you is the best way to face grief, preparing for the inevitability of grief is faith in you, and our best approach to live. Amen!

There are so many revelations that appear without expectations that one can only be thankful and blessed that Lord God Almighty is in control. I believe, without a doubt, that when we are aware of our status of who we are in Christ Jesus- all that is attacking us in a negative way will not prosper. Guilt, depression, anguish, pain, and loss will not find victory in those, who follow God in purpose, patience, endurance, and more importantly love. We the mourners, will be victorious and that my dear readers is the crux of revelation.

> *Psalm 90:1 Lord, you have been our dwelling place throughout all generations,*

> *Psalm 91 :1 Whoever dwells in the shelter of the Most High will rest in the shadow of the Almighty.*

such as those expressed. How could I ever have ascertained one moment of disbelief in our remarkable Savior, doubted He would bring me onward across my mountains of suffering to a place of flowing waters, and shower me in a peace beyond this world's recognition. There is no need to seek out method that will only fail in our attempt to doctor our own hurt. This action is never relevant to our healing, nor does it satisfy our scorched soul. The beauty of God's world continues and each star will twinkle down like an inspiring diamond in the universe and golden hues of sunlight will sweep the day among clouds of soft white images. Will we miss the substance of the falling rain or the icy fingers of winter before

We see clearly that life is a gift? Even when we have to pause in a difficult trial, which emerges suddenly and viciously in our life- will we truly recognize we have God Almighty in our corner? My Mom always told me "Haste makes waste" I never fully understood her meaning behind this message as a child. Now when I face trials in my life I remember these words and realize that the message conveyed is simply stated reflecting faith.- If we are to quick to turn away from God we may stand to lose what we have already built before our storm began. Use wisdom in every case and move cautiously. This is a substantial practice you the reader would be wise in adopting not only in faith, but with every daily situation you encounter.

My wonderful Mom always had lovely uplifting messages to offer at just the right moment when your world appeared confusing and cloudy. Another favorite of Mom's was "There will always be times of trouble and disappointment- that is life. I have learned to overcome obstacles by believing that each day something good will happen for me," When I was faced with mountains of horrific pain and loss why did I not apply this wise council to the shattering pages of my life ? Why did I not remember Mom's words of comfort and hope ? My only answer to negative response to my trials was because I never stopped on tracks of reality – truth did not matter-because denial exonerated me from any blame or error on my part of my nightmare.

I have come to realize truth is the ultimate difficulty to look at square in the face. You may try to cover truth with a falsehood, bury it deep in the confines of your mind, alter conditions that change circumstances, and dress up and masquerade a lie as truth, but in finality, you can put lipstick on a pig but it is still a pig- a deception and so was my denial.

Scripture reminds us that God hates liars and at Judgment will deal harshly with this sin. Recalling this forced me to walk away from my denial and accept what I had always known deep in my closet of rationale. My daughters were gone, because of their mistakes and choices. As I accepted these words- truth remained in light and glory as expected. I no longer had to fight dragons or bite bullets for I was finally free and logical for the first time since I entered my dark depression - a playground of death and loneliness. Amazing God had reached out and lifted me back from my portal of destruction. Yes, I missed my daughters more then words can express, but God's grace and mercy swiftly and gently embraced me and brought me to safety. I knew with certainty that I would one day see my daughters again. When doubt creeps its shadowy fingers over my thinking I remember

John 16:22 Now is your time of grief, but I will see you and rejoice, and no one will take away your joy. This is my promise I will see, hold, and be with Melanie and Lauren again. Praise and thanks to our God Almighty, who never forgets his children. Revelation of knowing God is always watching, and protecting us relieved all anxiety. I no longer had to watch and fear the serpent's sting. Now I had a warrior to do battle for me against my destructive forces of evil and I would have victory over my distraught soul because He lives.

> *Because He lives, I can face tomorrow,*
> *Because He lives, all fear is gone,*
> *Because I know – I know He holds the future,*
> *And life is worth the living-just because He lives.*
> *Composers. Bill and Gloria Gaither*

This beautiful Hymn expresses every positive aspect of the Lord God Almighty and assures us His majestic hold on our future is always in His hands- not in ours. Revelation of who He is and an everlasting protection for His children is a promise from Him that we never have to face our trials alone. When we face loss, grief, and desperation, we can be wise in knowledge of God and His forgiveness and more importantly, his love.

Dear God- Thank you for your outstretched arms you showed your prodigal daughter. I was lost and could not see truth as it appeared. I know now you showed mercy to Melanie and Lauren when you brought them back home to your safety. Thank you for never giving up on me or them. Always keep me safe using wisdom in all things- whatever the cost. With all my love, your daughter, Joan.

After that, revelations began to appear every day as I became stronger seeking out more of the wisdom of the Lord and making application of this wisdom to my daily routine. I no longer judged others for their actions pertaining to my grief. I no longer ran away from truth, or replaced it with falsehood. I accepted all, who chose to mourn with me- instead of brushing them away as one does wit first fresh fallen snow on a window sill. I forgave all,who had a part in their death and perhaps, that was the most honest and difficult revelation I had to face and endure. I remembered the envy I carried toward women,who had their children alive and well.

A shock in the face revelation for me as I read each word of my Bible. I remember how envy had destroyed me causing depression and inability to eat or sleep, which,consumed me with anger and hatred. I brought all envy to the Lord and he forgave me. I wonder sometimes if our revelations to our healing is right in front of us all the time, and we just are to caught up in our own drama to recognize the answer is and always has been right there in front of us. If we have to face our discoveries and confront our revelation to start healing, then would this not be a fuller and more productive existence then life in a bottle sealed in a forever time of no escape? When we are in doubt we lack all ability to grow and believing in faith is a remarkable and necessary step in the right direction to healing within

> *Matthew 21:22 iI you believe, you will receive whatever you ask for in prayer.*

Pray and follow God . He will according to his will grant your desires I emphasized this scripture,because this is a key promise from God. All you have to do is honor what He asks off us. Revelations of honor to God follows

> *Psalm 97:1 The Lord reigns; let the earth be glad; let the distant shores rejoice.*

> *Philippians 4:4 Rejoice in the Lord; always;I will say it again; Rejoice!*

> *Psalm 136:1 Give thanks to the Lord, for He is good.*

Psalm 28:7 The lord is my strength and my shield; my heart trusts in Him, and he helps me.

My heart leaps for joy, and with my song I praise him. James 4:8 Come near to God and He will come near to you.

There are many revelations throughout scripture that you can apply to your healing process. To many to number. It is my prayer that you will seek more of them as you read God's word.

Dear Lord, please bless each and every reader of this book with insight into revelation to promote their healing. Grant them wisdom to know how to apply these open doors to themselves and discern their appropriate choices guided by your infinite love and merciful hand of protection. Amen!! There is no right answer for everyone to follow, nor a pattern written in stone for mourners to grab hold for preservation of their self assurance.

Tomorrow is another day and we must press onward toward the prize. This just is and acceptance of our slow process of healing will ultimately bring hope for a near, clearer future filled with strength, understanding, and growth to our faith and lives.. We might experience great loss,,which turns us upside down tumbling into a spiral of emotions we never experienced.. Take heart dear reader as we need not to walk this shaky line of survival ourselves.

We have God Almighty to walk beside, in back, in front, above, and under us all the way till we are home free. My grief was mixed with so many different emotions I was all over the page. There were a multitude of lost moments where I could not-or would not acknowledge grief. I would smile through tears and want nothing more than to be invisible to all. God saved me from despair and I am so blessed He did for without his love and support I could have wasted away into oblivion and never returned to my family for life.

Psalm 30:1 I will extol you, Lord; for you lifted me out of the depths and did not let my enemies gloat over me.

When I began to understand, all personal blame disappeared and I entered a new day – one of promise and truth. This was a new concept for me to work with, and one that I proudly embraced with all my heart. I recalled scripture that clearly defined words of comfort during my period of grief and loss.

Job 121 "Naked I came from my Mother's womb,
And naked I swill depart.
The Lord gave and the Lord has taken away;
May the name of the Lord be praised."

I know this is exactly what my daughters would say to me if they were here now.

Each day is a new one- a special gift of life that should focus on His kingdom- not ours. For many families, Christmas is romantic, fun giving, sharing, loving, food festival event. A glorified and embellished season. I chose to elaborate on this special time, because once again, it is the reason for the season. As I write bright colors of the rainbow surface making their peek-a-boo debut in family dress- decorations on the lawn as passers by eye them maybe with intent to take an idea or two for their own, and all around the world music to soothe the savage beast.

I always loved Christmas until Lauren died. She took the beauty and happiness of the holiday with her. From that time on I would not and could not find joy, or religious time for honoring God. For miracles-where was mine? I tried Christmas Eve service, but could not concentrate on the message, or worship. Lauren has been gone since 2004 and my loss so unexpected-so cruel took a large chunk out of my heart and faith. It has been a slow and difficult process for my return to God and even more difficult in healing. I truly believe that this was due to experiencing Lauren's death while I was still reeling from Melanie's. Time is not the enemy. What happens within our life when a destructive force appears becomes our nemesis, but we have victory because of who He is – not who we are.

Revelation 1:8 ." I am the Alpha and the Omega-," says the Lord God," who is, and who was,and who is to come, the Almighty."

Amen Lord, Amen!!

I was always on a deadline and I prided myself for being organized and responsible. When a task ended and I needed to face other challenges. I rested in the secure knowledge that God is the keeper of our time and our time is a sign of God's love. My dearest reader-it doesn't get better than that!! Each new day is another chance to start again. When we recognize revelations referencing depressive circumstances, we no longer are standing in the gap waiting. This is the time when application of what we have learned is not silent -new information becomes a blessing- one we welcome with open arms as we grow in faith and wellness.. I call this last phase of healing - recovery. This may seem just a simple change of condition yet, this is the most important piece to your final step in this confusing, frustrating, painful, healing process.

Believe it or not, this is an important division of healing with family and friends . This is when a cup of kindness is needed the most as loved ones pour their support, encouragement, and most importantly, love over you as you seek your path to freedom. Intensive continual comfort springs forth, hope, love, and untangles your Jungle Gym of questions, and answers motioning you forward on your journey. Joy and success are just around your corner and old nemesis fear fades quickly from the scene.

Hostility and madness have taken flight and you stand solid in knowing you have conquered all that was impossible just through determination, faith, and endurance. No longer are you a resident of a desolate wasteland sinking in a quicksand of memories and sadness. To often we do not allow ourselves to think positive thoughts when we are caught up in grief. Opportunity for us is there all the time, but we deliberately ignore this, because the most difficult ways to follow are never the easiest to understand.. We just want easy however it comes. Nothing good ever comes easy my dear reader . You would do well to remember that as you move forward.

Simply stated ⁓easy is as easy goes and that is not the road you want to travel on. Your inability to forgive is now no longer a question for judgment of others is no longer harsh and interfering with your growth. As you become cognizant of where and how prayer plays a vitally important piece to your journey home your faith begins to bubble⁓as a pot of boiling water ready for contents to be placed within. Eager and watchful you begin to view everything in a shining light, rather than shadows of darkness and despair. You pray without ceasing and God hears and answers.

> *Proverbs 3:5⁓6 Trust in the Lord with all your heart and lean not on your own understanding; in all your ways submit to him and he will make your paths straight.*

The Lord answers not in a thunderous roar, but in a soft whisper so faint⁓one has to be quiet and listen carefully to not miss His message. If any of you lack wisdom; this would be the time to advance your petitions and requests before Him. Wisdom is granted to all, who seek God and is graciously bestowed to everyone for God is not a respecter of persons . Errors are not a consideration in God's eyes⁓ if you are faithful God will bless you greatly. Wisdom will be a key milestone in our first revelation as we assume our final steps on our path to freedom.

RECOVERY/REACHING THE SUMMIT

Grief provides the battleground for guilt. As we have just learned in our previous chapter wisdom is a vital component to identify grief and understanding grief supports healing and hope in case of a horrific loss. I was able to apply my lessons learned to shelter my double dilemma of sadness, which engulfed my wounded soul in a most profound manner. At a workshop for grief I found many people, who experienced guilt throughout their grief. Rationale for their emotions covered a wide range of excuses. People found themselves a central cause of their loss or a failure in preventing the inevitable. Past words and deeds said and done were filled with regret.

Acting as the jury and rendering the decision to disconnect their lifeline were viewed as second guesses. Many were consumed with anger, relief,apathy, and even out of place laughter. Of course, God was to blame always. This was much easier than facing giants by ourselves. Grief provides a solid ground for guilt, but now here come revelations marching through the door to enlighten you with real truth .Guilt is almost always irrational.

I remember my early thinking if I had only taken Melanie to our Pastor's home that night when she asked me to she would be alive today. I was blaming myself in a way that made no sense. Eventually she would have returned to her home and the events of the next day still would have happened. Guilt is often buried inside This takes the subtle form of What if, should have, and if only. I was her mom and I should have stopped her that day when she came to my home. I did' not see or hear the peril in her voice or actions as I let her go. I had paid more attention I could have stopped the nightmare before it took flight.

Grief forms from unrealistic expectations.

I truly believed that even though I was teaching and working as a single mom responsible for my children and aging parents- I should have spent more time with Melanie. Maybe then I could have saved her. After she died- I tried to be perfect to everyone in my life and felt my unrealistic expectations spitting me in half so I was not even able to save myself.

Guilt can distort facts

Guilt most definitely made me see through rose colored glasses instead of clarity of reason. I reached out for Melanie time and time again, and when I failed to reach her overwhelming guilt fell smack on top of me. If I had been more cognizant of my emotions I would have seen a very different portrait. Was I destroying myself to reach out to someone, who did not want to be reached? Simply stated, who was the foolish one here-me or Melanie. Maybe, in some small way we both missed that boat. All that I was left with was an empty wallet and a pocketful of tears.

Guilt is usually over things we cannot change

How many times Melanie wanted to go for a walk, shop, or just learn the Piano. Why did I almost always answer her with " sorry honey – I have to many things to do – maybe another time " Perhaps, if I had taken more of my time to spend with her she would not have felt so abandoned. Well dear reader- here is a monumental revelation for you to digest. Guilt is not designed to be a permanent and consistent emotion, but rather a temporary condition signaling a warning that we have an error to correct. Death and loss cannot be a rewind for us to consider. When we think we can and can't-guilt steps down into our life causing us great burden, which prevents God from healing us. Here is a step methods to assist you in freeing yourself from guilt.

First and most importantly you must identify and admit your guilt.

Guilt becomes a loaded time bomb when we don't recognize this feeling in us .Identifying guilt enables us to visualize how hurtful we become to ourselves.

Secondly- Talk about your guilt,

Be honest with yourself. You will never let go of your guilt until you recognize that the more you talk and release your pain you will not be able to let go.

Third- Write about your guilt.

Sometimes, when we view our reason/s in black and white there is a more realistic perception of ours behind our emotions. Writing often to your loved one may be less difficult to do then facing someone one on one with made up rationale. Difficulty to talk with someone is replaced by your logic.

Fourth- Recognize that you are human.

There is only one perfect one and we know him to be without blemish. He is Jesus and perfection. We are faulty humans, who make mistakes and do things we regret and so did our loved ones. This inability to be perfect does not deem us as horrible people- just human.

Fifth- Forgive yourself.

You may have difficulty forgiving yourself, which may block your ability to feel God's forgiveness, and God'[s forgiveness sets us free. As noted in Amazing Grace

Amazing grace! How sweet the sound
That saved a wretch like me:
I once was lost, but now am found;
Was blind, but now I see.

Composer John Newton

Six- View your guilt as someone else would.

I believe this was an area I failed in completely. I found strength with helping others in the same pain I had, yet, I could not or would not look at myself as a third person to understand my expectations of myself were unrealistic. Why would I not give myself the same honesty as I gave to others? Why would I blame my self when I was teaching them not to take any blame? If my compassion was bestowed on others why not myself as well? What an important revelation that was when I realized this.

Seven- Recall the good that you did.

If we become saturated with guilt, we end up tangled in a web of negativity. Our minds become saddled with painful memories . Now is the time to start replacing negative thoughts for every positive thing we accomplished with or for our loved one. A freshly born insight into a stream of positive memoirs and events you shared together. Recognize good- accept your commendation.

Lastly-- embrace the living.

If you struggle with guilt then turn your "if only" into "next time"Things you wished you had done- words you wished you had said; say or do these now for those living in your life. Make the change and give yourself a second opportunity to reach out and make it count.

There is no set blueprint or any other means where you can clearly look at your short comings in your grief then these eight revelations we now have in place to follow through on a successful journey for recovery. Dissolving guilt leads to healing and healing ourselves in every aspect of our life is what this book's mission reflects. As we gain further insight into healing and recovery, we realize that under God's grace and hand of mercy forgiveness reigns. If God can forgive us- surely we can forgive ourselves!

Coping with our loneliness may be overwhelming and a dangerous area to walk.. Loneliness after grief settles may be the very culprit that wipes you out preventing your moving on. Loneliness for me was just that where I felt enclosed in a cave with no exits and no light .The more I tried to escape- deeper in this cage I would go. Silence builds to a point where you just turn on television. What is on is not important- another voice with you is. Often after hours when programs were over I would watch news till I fell asleep. No one to share any excitement with, call and discuss my day, or look forward to card on mother's day, Christmas, birthdays, or any other remarkable celebrations with friends and family to share through years to come.

We in turn, may withdraw from others as well. Our reasons may be perhaps from past hurtful statements conveyed to us, or we feel unfaithful to our loved one if we try to enjoy ourselves socially. We may feel like we are poor company for others, or we may just not have any energy left within us to socialize at this point. Whatever the reason, we must for our own sake take a breath and move forward back into life, and more importantly, know with certainty that God will always be by your side.

Hebrews 13:5 "Never will I leave you; never will I forsake you."

Because isolation can lead to despair, depression, or physical issues you need to guard yourself from all these negative conditions by reaching out to others through church meetings and group therapy. Don't for any reason push yourself into things you just are not ready for, but at the same time don't hold yourself back. Grief is pain and loneliness is a crossroad in the grief landscape. Grief comes in and out like the ebbing of the ocean tide. Sometimes, when least expected a huge wave will surface and knock you off your feet.

Grief is filled with backward and forward movements. Sometimes, you feel as if your sliding backward when in fact you are healing. Embrace this emotion, take it in, and let the upsurges occur. This is necessary for your well being- just let your tears flow and know this is the most healing thing you can have. Having upsurges of grief is a positive reaction. This means you are human.

Sometimes we experience upsurges,which bring to mind memories of our loved ones.

When I returned to church, certain songs would bring tears to my eyes. I feel deep sadness remembering, yet, when I did I could visualize my two daughters sitting beside me in worship. At any special event music fills me with both a mixture of joy and sadness as memories pour forth like cascading clouds over a dark sky now in beauty and light.

Lord God I pray that I may never grow one day older without remembering my two beautiful daughters you gave to me. May I always hear and remember funny jokes and times we shared. May I never forget how to smile through tears when my thoughts are of them, or speak of them with pride and gratitude for being their mom and sharing their lives. Thank You-.Amen. There are a multitude of questions you will be faced with and most of them will center around timing issues relative to when you should do things. Changes are always different for each person and timing is never the same. When to do what is a personal decision relative to putting your loved ones clothes away, cleaning a closet out, and just mentioning their name. Depending on circumstances, each person has a unique list of what needs to be done. Some changes that need to be addressed such as insurance policies, and legal or financial documents may dictate your timing response in your decision making. If you lack in decision making- speak to a good friend or family member for confirmation on your required action.

> *Ecclesiastes 3:1 There is a time for everything, and a season for every activity under the heavens*

What we need to do is seek out and find our timing and then fine tune this to our activities we engage in- seems fairly simple, but in reality a complex action, which needs to be nurtured and acted upon with careful thought and appropriate response, Believe it or not, speaking with others assists you in getting out any painful feelings that remain from any action you have to take. Above all confusion, follow your hear t. What about prayer?

Within grief support groups, there are individuals,who pray out of necessity and there are those, who are angry at God. This does not mean that one Christian is better than the other., or holds a stronger faith in God. Simply stated- here is a Christian, who finds prayer easy to face as opposed to a . Christian, who may find prayer difficult to relate to. Every person is different in preparation for moving forward- not just in timing, but also with understanding. There are many reasons for an individual to not desire to pray/

They may be physically or emotionally exhausted, difficulties in communicating,consumed with to much guilt to pray, new to prayer and cannot decide how to begin,,plagued with doubt so they feel praying would be hypocritical, and others, who tell them it is necessary to pray, and hearing this convicts you to try. When you fail, this is as if you are pouring salt on an open wound

As I have said many times throughout this book, application of lessons we learn is a key point to successful healing of our unshakable torment and suffering. Walking with God is our only save. Some times we are blessed in understanding what it means to walk with God.. I was in the percentile of those,who were aware of God himself- but had no idea of what walking with God entailed. Desiring to know how to walk, I returned to scripture and sought answers.

1 John 1-7 But if we walk in the light, as he is in the light, we have fellowship with one another, and the blood of Jesus, his Son, purifies us from all sin.

1 John 2-6 Whoever claims to live in him must live as Jesus did.

Our dark times may also be times God wants to teach us something more about ourselves and His love for us providing we wait patiently, and trust God's heart- desire to design us in that light. You know when least expected- there it is- saltine crisp shining brightly before our eyes. My answer- clear and right on target. We must listen closely to God's voice when trouble comes raging through our door and agony strikes and crushes our life. God is faithful and remains close to those, who are deeply wounded. I had turned away from God while He never let me go-always watching from a distance-patient, compassionate, and loving.

Tragedy or testing, dark days and dreary nights, God knows what we are facing and is concerned. I realized that losing my two children was the lowest and saddest point of my life and that Almighty God is with us in our sorrow. Sorrow can cause us to doubt God's plan and ask questions that should never be considered such as has God forgotten his promises- failed for all time? Has God chosen to not be merciful? Has God in anger retaliated withholding His compassion. Though we may face trouble, and difficulties, sadness,and pain- God is still in control and he is always with us

We need to return to Him in faith and call on Him for strength. Why? Because whether we face death, discouragement, loss, or pain, we can take great comfort in knowing that no sorrow is to deep that God cannot feel it with us. God wants to help deliver us from it. He wants to bring us his divine comfort. Try an arrow prayer. These prayers are short and sweet composed of a single thought or phrase, which you shoot straight up to the sky as if you were using a bow and arrow.. This is powerful whenever you feel a need to pray and no energy to do so. You may also just yell " HELP" another powerful – quick prayer. God will know what you need. Above all be totally honest with God. Let him know your pain,guilt,anger,disappointment,abandonment, or anything else on your heart.

> *Psalm6:9 tells us clearly The Lord has heard my cry for mercy:*
> *the Lord accepts my prayer.*

Just be in God's presence resting quietly and listen to your thoughts. If one strikes you that appears one you need to share with God, then do so

Certain thoughts are prayers. There are monument moments when whatever the attitude of the body, the soul is on its knees. Whenever I have difficulty in praying I draw comfort from scripture.

In the same way, the Spirit helps us in our weakness. We do not know what we ought to pray for, but the Spirit himself intercedes for us with groans. that words cannot express. And he who searches our heart knows the mind of the Spirit, because the Spirit intercedes for the Saints according with God's will.

I have learned I am not perfect but I am loved. My grief never stayed in place. Every time I emerged from a phase, I would fall into a repeat pattern going. round and round.. There were changes where I felt as if I were on a spiral, but my only problem with that was I could not decipher if I was spiraling up or down, I have learned in all certainty that we are healed of a suffering only when we experience it in full. There is no way around your suffering when someone you love has died. Understand here this is a natural feeling. There is no way to go over, under, or around it. Acceptance and going through grief is the only way you will find healing.

> *Matthew 5:4 Blessed are those who mourn, for they will be comforted,*

You are the one grieving, so what anyone else thinks or says is not important. At this stage of your life -you need to grieve. Don't try to fight or control it. Just breathe and grieve. Grief is pretty much all-encompassing, so I believe that although, not everyone may be affected in all the following areas – I do think many o f these issues are felt in great suffering.

Psychologically or emotionally

This the most obvious way grief slams you, however, many of the emotions felt may be strange or never felt before. Riding out my painful feelings was the most important step I had to make in my healing process.

Socially

If your loss surrounds an integral connection to your personal and professional standing- you may lose your self confidence and relationships with others, You may even lose total friendships as others pull away from you. I know that happened when I lost my two daughters and as painful as that was losing friends and family just escalated my anger drawing me into a deeper pit of loneliness.

Spiritually

Sometimes faith sustains, and often, there may be a period of assessing faith as you know it. For me, I felt completely abandoned, which was a turning point in my healing. I needed to wrap my arms around my girls,but they were gone beyond reach and so was God. At least, this is what I thought till I reached a bit further and took baby steps back into faith and loving arms.

By acknowledging my anguish I was able to look square in the face of pain and beyond. I have come to understand and recognize God's presence in even the most grievous of situations.

Physically

Physically our bodies suffer multiple blows, which impacts every aspect of our normal functioning both inside and outside our bodies. I can only attribute everything I experienced to my grief, which drew me down like quicksand into unforgettable physical issues. I had breathing problems where my chest felt weighed down and I was not breathing at all. Other times, I felt as if my breathing was to shallow and I would become dizzy and experience pounding headaches. My weight was like an elevator up and down. I could not sustain one solid weight, and in and out Doctor's offices with complaints and aches only to find deep anxiety was the culprit causing everything wrong resulting from horrific grief. Releasing my pain healed my body.

Mentally

Mentally I was absent minded, accident prone, showed difficulty with concentration, and had very slow responses, which placed me into a dangerous fog of grief ultimately resulting in, car and other accidents. After some understanding how grief was destructive, I re-thought my steps and embraced my new found freedom to recovery.. Becoming overwhelmed was my downfall and so I pass these pearls of wisdom along to those, who are now where I once was. Don't bury your demons- confront them.

Crying

Anyone, who has witnessed a healing of addiction, a love story beyond all expectations, or an unexpected gift knows how to shed tears of joy, relief, gratitude, so why not tears of sadness? They matter too. Some have difficulty producing tears in the presence of others, while others cry at the drop of a hat. This has to do greatly with a person's sensitive nature which is innate. Circumstances don't dictate here. When all is said and done- the bottom line is crying touches the soul, crying is the entrance to healing, and crying is recovery. People must be given an opportunity to hurt out loud.

Holidays

There is no possible way of avoiding firsts or prevent them from hurting. Holidays are most difficult firsts to face- in my case, they were a double wound to my already shattered heart. Holidays steeped with tradition, gatherings of friends and family, sharing gifts, and good food were always a joy for me to look forward to with peace, and relaxation -for I never minded shopping or preparation. This became my crowning presentation- trying to do my very best as a hostess welcoming guests to our home. My favorite holidays were Christmas and Easter unfortunately, both celebrations were forever destroyed when Melanie died on Easter and Lauren on Christmas.

There are no explanations for me as to why these tragedies occurred on these particular holidays, nor is there any rationale I can equate to the fact that I am writing this particular portion of my book now- at Christmas- with all the merry and busy associated with this very special time for family and friends. I guess this time was meant to be part of my healing process- as you will learn in recovery you are always healing for that never stops. The difference is that each healing episode becomes easier and less intense than the last onset of a painful memory. What is the cost of a loss may depend entirely on where your loved one fit in your life pattern. If you lost a parent- that would be a very different ballgame than one you would experience with a loss sustained from a death of a child,sibling, or friend.

I know only to well all impacts are horrific,but in essence so very different. Before I lost Melanie, I was blind sighted by loss of my Mom and my Dad- I guess you could say that within two years I had lost four precious members of my immediate family, and life as I once knew it was dark and lonely. I often think of this loving scripture which holds victory for me in understanding how much he loves us.

> *Isaiah 43 :1 But now, this is what the Lord says he who created you, Jacob, he who formed you, Israel, "Do not fear, for I have redeemed you; I have summoned you by name; you are mine. I Have summoned you by name; you are mine.*

What and how you handle your first year of loss will be a first serious step in this long healing process, but do not be discouraged—all that you do the first year may and certainly does not need to be done in the same manner year after year. I have found my periods of remembering are so much lighter then I focus on their life and not on my grief. In your measure of preparation keep or change your traditions, laugh and smile if you desire, and last—if you feel led to cry—then cry. Handling holidays is no easy task and no one person has the same need. You make the decisions, decide what and where your needs fall, and then graciously communicate these needs to those around you.We will never know God's perfect timing, but it certainly is His timing—not ours and we need to be cognizant of His world, not ours. I would have loved to have spent more time with my two daughters this certainly was not in the deck of cards I held. Almighty God is maker of heaven and earth. We have no power as great as He—therefore, why fight what is past, embrace your present and let go of an inner desire to reverse time—as this fantasy will only lead you further down a path of despair and no return.

Dear reader, not one of us knows the rough bumpy terrain we may encounter, but our loving God does. His footsteps are always beside us. Never think He is not when you see only your prints in the sand. This beautiful poem tells us God/s compassion for His children is perfection.

Footprints

One night I dreamed a dream.
I was walking along the beach with my Lord.
Across the dark skies flashed scenes from my life.
For each scene, I noticed two sets of footprints in the sand
One belonging to me, and one to my Lord.
When the last scene of my life shot before me,
I looked back to the footprints in the sand, and to my surprise,
I noticed that many times along the path of my life,

By Mary Stevenson

This poem tells it all. God never abandons us. Amen!!!!!

God has, is, and always will be with us forever here in this depraved world we live in as long as we breathe. He forgives us when we meet Him and decide to follow Him wherever He leads. He brings mercy like soft dewdrops on the first Rose and His grace – abundantly bestowed on His children. He loves us unconditionally through trials and protects our choices~ even when we are wrong. He is Sovereign, He is the Christ, He is Almighty God!!!!

Part Four: Summit

Mountain High: Healing of the Heart: Rebuilding

Graduation Day: Congratulations

Grief is normal, natural and necessary to your healing process. You have suffered a great loss- one which is indescribable to others. Only you feel the shattering of your life. Others may try to comfort you during this period of loss- they may even claim they know what you are feeling. They say the words, but in reality- they cannot know your devastation unless they themselves have walked in your shoes. There is no need for you to apologize when your whole world has collapsed and the hole in your heart is so deep you cannot begin to know where to start mending .

The Bible speaks:

Revelation 21:4-5

"He will wipe every tear from their eyes. There will be
no more death or mourning, or crying, or
pain, for the old order of things has passed away." He
who was seated on the throne said," I am
making everything new!"

I have to believe that scripture for this allows me to see beyond their death. All the incriminating, psychological, emotional, daze, confusion garbage is lifted at that moment and all I see before me is a promise that God has made my daughters whole again- new. I smile and thank him for His mercy and my healing. This is not a daydream. This is as real as you could possibly imagine. Instead of fixing your eyes on your pain and suffering, choose to live in secure knowledge that one day God's restoration project will bring hope and new life. God never promised to remove our pain. Instead, He offers us His grace to guide us through our suffering.

I have come to understand that death is just a passing into another time-another place. When I look at my photographs of my two daughters It feels as if they are saying to me Mom, I have only slipped away to another room. I am still I and you are still you. Whatever we were to each other-we still have that connection. Death leaves a heartache no one can heal, but love leaves a memory no one can steal.a never ending relationship. Death ends a life From out of my pain, God became a living reality to me as I had never experienced .before.

I continued to trust in God,because even in my darkest and deepest pit, I knew with certainty that through His grace I would live again. We begin to rebuild our lives, but rebuilding does not begin in earnest until you have walked and sifted through your sand pile of memories, and regrets, consumed fires of anger and guilt, and rested in strong determination of hope and healing. Rebuilding does not happen instantaneously, on the contrary, rebuilding our life is slow based on multiple factors, which include time and energy you spent in grief, relationship to the departed, timing and circumstances surrounding your loss, and how strong your outside support is encouraging you. To move forward.

You may face challenges associated with change, but embrace them for each change will catapult you to another level in your healing process. Change is difficult.- some more than others require. I imagined their voices laughing- and each street I passed held a vision of them riding bikes, swimming in the ocean, and running up and down our stairs prepared for school. This all was to much for me in the same home I brought them to and watched them grow. Moving away did help channel some of my pain, but led me to a new area of adjustment

I was not ready for. I left everyone I knew- friends and family even my employment, and settled for loneliness as a stranger with difficult decisions to make. Some changes are temporary, but mine were major decisions I could not change back. I would caution you on jumping from a pot into a fire. Take your time and make changes that are significant to your well being and not detrimental with new regrets.

I deeply miss my Boston, but I have learned to adjust to a new life in the deep south one day at a time. Abraham Lincoln always believed that the best thing about the future was that it only comes one day at a time. You would be wise to adopt this very knowledgeable President's philosophy and practice this wisdom to ease your sorrow. Wounds do not heal over night, anymore than a wound to our flesh-as this manifests in many stages. Healing emotional wounds also heal in degrees. Healing can and may cause an unexpected burden to your life

If you desire to cry -then cry for this helps to heal your soul. The pain passes but the beauty will forever remain. Dear God I trust in you. Please help me in my many moments of doubt and distrust. Thank you Lord, Amen!. Healing is the most majestic hike you will ever take. At the end of the journey you will find rest and restoration. A new self will emerge- one you may not recognize, but you will accept with enthusiastic joy, hope, and more importantly love. A love that knows no bounds as scripture once again tells us

Corinthians 13:7-8

Love always protects
always trusts,
always hopes,
always perseveres,
love never fails.

As you encounter changes in your life, remember you are the only one with your hand on the buzzer and when you are ready- you will make that decision. Take time-weigh all positives against negatives and when your positives out weigh your negatives then- and only at that moment- hit your buzzer and move forward on your journey of change. Don't allow anyone to pressure or rush you. When the time is right, you will know, and step in confidence on the stairs to recovery.

Anniversaries are perhaps the most difficult periods of memories we need to face after our love ones have gone. I would consider myself negligent to these writings if I told you I sail through Anniversaries, because simply stated, I do not. Each Christmas and Easter are still my most painful times I face each year. However, I will tell you in all honesty- that each year my pain is replaced remembering their lives by doing something special those times and then- there is unspeakable joy in memory as I celebrate these holidays

Reaching out to others wiping their tears brings healing to our heart and paves a new path in our direction for recovery. St. Francis of Assisi believed by giving freely to another we will reap rewards of jubilation. A young woman I met had lost a child at birth. Although, she mourned deeply for her loss she began to reach out to other Moms, who shared her grief. As she soothed each tear her aching heart was starting to mend. The more she was able to minister to others and help their pain and loss- her own heart played a new song. She returned to school and became a Pastor for women and shared her testimony of healing to others. It helps to see how good overcomes sorrow.

Look into your heart and if and when you believe time is approaching for you to step up to the plate and serve others grief struck- then go for it!!Those, who suffer from a loss need people, who truly care, no one understands more than those, who have walked the walk of sorrow, and always remember when one ministers there is always a double benefit received. Helping others should never become a task from obligation, or an assignment to make yourself feel better. This should only develop from your heart's desire to minister- and for no other reason.

Some people may believe that if they move forward that would be most disrespectful to their departed. This always happens as you approach Graduation Day. You have done so well with your baby steps to a new freedom and now comes a sledge hammer to deconstruct what you have so faithfully built .I have only words of wisdom for consolation to you at this time. Even if you feel you have a long way to go be proud of each goal you reach. God is with you each step of the way and I am too. In words of Helen Keller- what we have once enjoyed and deeply loved we can never lose for all we have loved deeply becomes a part of us.

> *Jeremiah 31:13 I will turn their mourning into gladness:; I will give them comfort and joy instead of sorrow."*

> *Genesis 28:15 I am with you and will watch over you wherever you go, and I will bring you back to this land.*

Rebuilding your life never means you have shattered all memory of your loved one's existence. You have no more abandoned them then God has abandoned His children. You may be shattered – not abandoned. You no longer are required to baby sit any guilt which you carry, and your loved one would want you to move forward in life, therefore, take a deep breath, embrace life and know with certainty your loved one will always hold an exceptional place in your heart and life.

Memories are like a re-run of old time movies where you needed a tissue box beside you to wipe away each tear a scene brought to your emotions, or a good reading novel which reminded you of your story. Yeah, memories are like that!

If you still hold painful memories the very best thing you can do for yourself is to practice what I refer to as the three A's of memory fallout.

1. Acknowledge- don't dismiss your feeling of pain,
2. Acclaim them – work with this sorrow

3. Achieve your result by resolving your issues

Then laugh and live again. Even the saddest memories can reflect peace, wisdom, and strength once we come to understand our rationale behind our pain..Memories hurt, memories help, memories heal/ I remember my girls Melanie and Lauren with love that is almost joy- lost and all mine- all mine forever.

On this your Graduation day I pray for Almighty
God to bless you in every aspect of your life
I pray for your continued healing and your ministry of healing others.
I pray for bouquets of daisies and laughter of exceeding joy.
I pray for forever a peace beyond all understanding.
I pray most importantly for love to surround you
I pray for your grieving heart to mend

Ecclesiastes 3:4
There is a time to weep, and a time to laugh, a
time to mourn, and a time to dance.

This author prays you choose to dance!!!!

EPILOGUE

Loss, and grief are natural occurrences in life. These predators rob joy and peace from our already complicated lives. More often than not, their appearance is swift, unchangeable, and deadly. Circumstances around acceptance of major tragedy and final separation depend largely on state of mind, strength of character, and personal acceptance. For those, who rode an emotional roller coaster as I did, acceptance was almost impossible yet,Jesus reached out and healed me of every emotional and physical bruise assaulted on my soul.

My beloved potter took this crumbling clay in hand, molding me into a humble, strong,independent,challenging, servant Evangelist Pastor for God. Jesus helped me make sweet lemonade from the sour lemons life dealt me. He taught me to bend in the wind as the tall reed in a storm, laugh at impossible, and use fierce intent attacking the improbable. He brought me truth and discernment for wisdom and commissioned me to break chains and set captives free. Jesus healed me of every stronghold keeping me down and brought me up to heights where young Eagles fly.

From 2000-2004 my loss was unspeakable and only through my faith in God I was able to move forward. In abundant joy, I am charged with a quest I will complete first for Christ and then my children. " A Dream For Melanie," who decided to break chains, set captives free, and retribution for Lauren, who never had a chance to climb and soar like an Eagle. This has now become my quest to fulfill their objectives. All ingredients of an authentic Roman stage drama played major tragedy in their brief lives, but I am their Mom and will not let their lives be in vain. AS I attain each goal before me and reach the summit of every unmovable mountain, I look up and thank God for all His blessings and am confident that from a distance He is always watching and waiting patiently.

Thank You- for allowing me to be your guide throughout your most difficult times. You and I share a common bond with Almighty God who grants me wisdom along our rocky journey seeking peace and recovery. My soul cries for you and prays for God to heal each bleeding wound and scar you have endured along this journey. As redemption, love, and healing occurs, just walk on with hope in your heart and never look back. I have seen the dark side of yesterday and have been introduced to bright hope for tomorrow through Jesus Christ. Each day His forgiveness empowers me as I wake to new challenges before me, and I feel truly blessed that He believes in me, for that alone soothes my soul and charges me with energy and purpose.

When I see a cloud above indicating rain, I am assured that whatever this rain brings I will have victory for I am in Christ and He is in me forever. I remember Melanie and Lauren's laughter, the special times we shared, and that alone brings joy to my soul.

"*I Remember Me*"

I remember long ago
When everything was new
Hope and joy were living then
And dreams could still come true

But I remember long ago
When I was still my own
Joy was forced to move away

And hope was left alone

And I remember long ago
That black and mournful day
When sadness came, and with it, pain
And drove dear hope away

Yes, I remember, long ago
How desperately I cried
When I learned one day to my dismay
That hope and joy had died

Still, I remember both of them
And the days when we were free
Yes, and I remember happiness
And I remember me

Melanie Rachelle (Beloved Daughter) Deceased

May the Lord grant you peace, understanding and love. May He shine down blessing every aspect of your life as you walk your journey to recovery.

REFERENCES

The Holy Bible: New International Version Zondervan Publishers (2011)

Sometimes it Rains: Breaking Chains of Bondage (2013) Dr. Joan Rathe

Breaking Chains Foundation and Ministry Publishing United States of America

Bible Promises for You Broad Street Publishing (2014) Racine, Wisconsin

Shattering Your Strongholds By Liberty Savard (1992) Bridge Logos Publishers-New Brunswick, New Jersey

Confessions Of a Grieving Christian By Zig Ziglar (2011)

Addendum

Exactly two days after I finished this book I received a telephone call from my only surviving child, Riva, who lives in Massachusetts. My excitement of finishing this very important testimonial came crashing to a sudden halt as I listened to her first sentence- "Mom" I am going to say something and no matter what, we have to trust God" "I sent you a picture of something and I want you to look at it" From the sound of her voice, I knew something was coming I did not want to hear. I held my breath as I looked and asked her. She hesitated and then blurted out in one quick statement that rocked my world of peace and joy.. "I have been diagnosed with Colon Cancer and I need to have surgery"

I suddenly felt as if I were hit once again with the same truck that ran over me twice before with the death of my other two daughters. What was happening here. We had a brief conversation and she agreed to keep us informed with every decision and step she took. "Mom, we have to walk this out and trust God" was her final statement before she ended the call. Was I upset? Did I cradle my head in my hands and cry bitter tears? Yes, to all of this. I was devastated, yet, my trust in God was solid. I thought of why and how- which was futile to waste my time on . That night I tossed and turned till I finally fell into a sound sleep. When I woke, the day seemed endless with chores which kept my mind distracted. Riva and I had talked that morning as she explained she would be telling her four children within the next two days. Because she had such a peace about her situation, I knew God was in control. I looked upward and prayed for His mercy and grace to touch her

> *Dear God, thank you for my Daughter, Riva. I want you to know God that I trust you completely in this situation and I love you with all my heart. I want you to know that no matter what happens here- I will always love you. I will never ever turn from you or leave you. What ever your decision Is I will always love and trust you forevermore. Amen. God still holds His pencil in His hand-He is not through writing my story.. Your Obedient Daughter--Joan*

When we understand who we are in Christ, we begin to understand His mind in clarity. First and most importantly, His love is for all His children Finally, to never forget that God sees everything we do, say, or think.

Although, there is a time appointed for judgment, He will discipline us for breaking His rules while we are here on planet Earth. Though our disobedience may not be felt till later on in our lifetime- each trial we face is because God allowed this to happen. Throughout the Bible Almighty God destroys Kings, towns, property, and families for dis-honoring Him. When we feel as if we will break from our trial- He steps in, forgives us, and wipes us whiter than snow. If we are intelligent enough to grasp an understanding that when He passes judgment on us for a previous offense is to make us aware He is God and although, He will forgive us – He will not allow us to repeat over again the same behavior. He will turn away and let us reap what we sow.

God is not a respecter of persons. Everyone is treated the same manner and no one escapes His authority or judgment. He has the whole world in His hands and that alone should reveal His majesty. From the first day we breathe as newborns we are born with a sinful nature and there is not one, who has not sinned at some point of their lifetime. As I mentioned in this book, grief is a puzzle we need to understand how this fits in our circumstances of loss before we are able to move forward to healing and recovery.

God too has our life in a pattern of design, which is supposed to elevate our multitude of His blessings and place us on paths toward victory. Unfortunately, our sins block our way and we fall flat on our face perplexed, angry, and depressed. When you realize God Almighty's character is not to see us in pain or need, we can place total blame on ourselves for our troubles and work toward a viable solution. Everything God says in scripture is TRUTH. Jeremiah 29:11 "for I know the plans I have for you" says the Lord. "plans to give you a hope and a future." God has a puzzle with pieces of our life in front of Him. When we travel another way God moves our life to fit his design. Missing pieces within our framework results from ourselves and choices we make along our lifetime. To often, our choices are vulnerable, intrinsic, and disastrous. We place ourselves in roles we choose, which prove not always the best.. God never changes~ we do. The book of. Revelation tells us He does not accept those, who defy His law. Almighty God is very clear on who will not be included.

> *Revelation 22:15 Outside are the dogs, those who practice magic arts, the sexually immoral, the murderers, the idolaters and everyone who loves and practices falsehood.*

When we veer off course Almighty God removes the pieces and construct another plan. The more we change for the better God enlarges our territory and showers us with blessing beyond expectation. Our lives are a puzzle composed of each facet and time frame throughout our existence. Sinning may be as simple as telling a small lie. To God, this is still considered a sin. When we attempt to fit in with the rest of the crowd, you may knowingly or unknowingly suppress the real you due to characteristics of the role model around you. This is a false assumption of who you truly are.

You may reflect sensuality and indulgence and reject acts of kindness, love, and submit to authority. You cam knockdown and block out good characteristics because of fear and rejection in your lifeline. Being friendly and trusting others is replaced with another personality that ushers in distrust, separation, and selfishness. Your new personality now is focused on distrust, and independence. When anyone of your senses is indulged in sin, the body is defiled.

There are 10 steps to overcoming and picking up your missing pieces to perfect the puzzle Lord God

Almighty intended in His design for your lifetime..

1. Submission to God
2. Truth at the Origin
3. Clear Your Identity
4. Come Into Right Standing With God and Yourself
5. Conversation With God
6. Rebuke the Enemy
7. Choose Love Over Judgment
8. Bring Action Into Alignment
9. Come into right standing With Man
10. Clear Vision Going Forward

Dear Reader,

Remember your loved ones with dignity and purpose. Remember the Fruits of the Spirit and apply them every day God blesses you with. Remember to move cautiously throughout each step not in haste but in love and understanding of your trials. Remember to praise and thank God for each blessing received and when you reach your summit raise your hands up high and shout praises of thanks.

Most importantly always remember who God is. He is the Christ the Lord God Almighty

> *"I am the Alpha and the Omega, the First and the Last, the Beginning and the End" (Revelation 22:13)*

"He is The Great I Am"
Now, You Are Becoming Unstoppable !

Printed in the United States
By Bookmasters